Key Stage 2

Science

SATS Practice Papers

Levels 3-5

Pack Contains:
Three full sets of SATS practice papers
Answer book with mark scheme and hints
(112 pages in all)

SCIENCE
KEY STAGE 2

Practice Paper 1
Test B

45 MINUTES

TOTAL SCORE

FIRST GO:

SECOND GO:

THIRD GO:

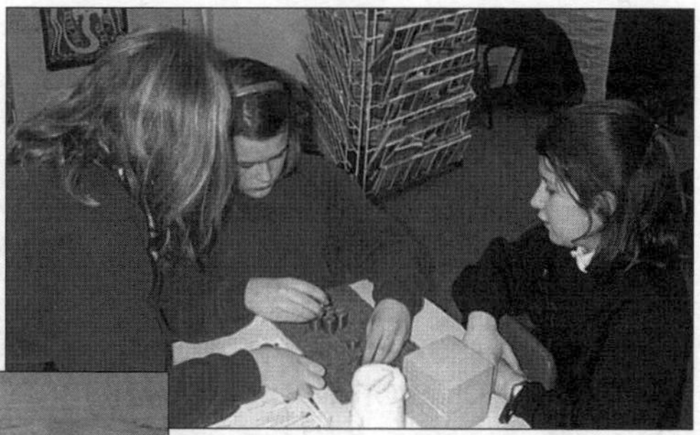

FIRST NAME

LAST NAME

SCHOOL

CGP

1 **Anatomy**

Sonya and Kirsty carried out an investigation to test whether adults' heads are bigger than children's heads.

Results were as follows:

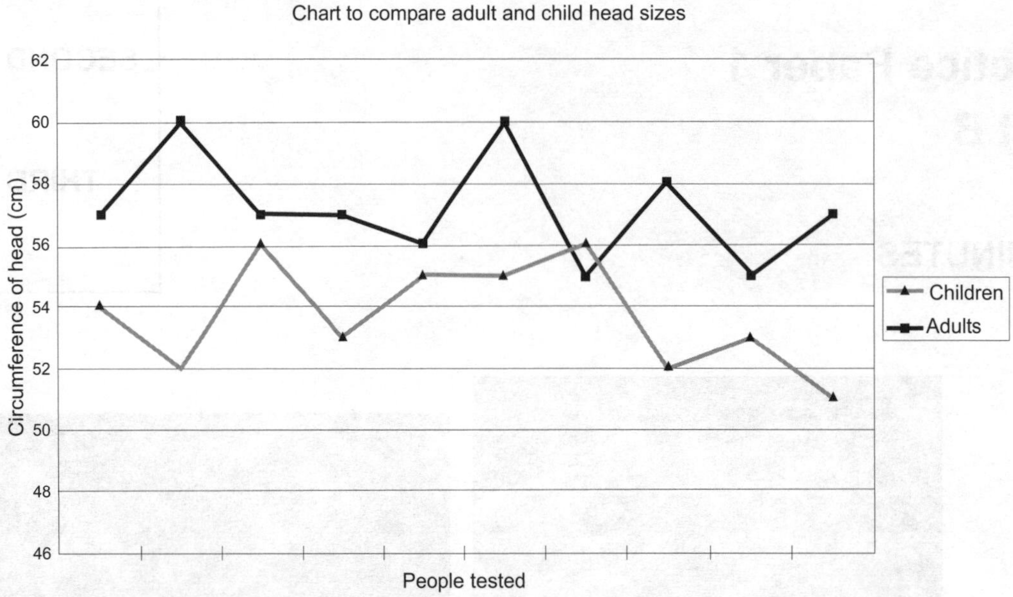

a) **What conclusion could you draw from these results?**

1 mark

....

....

b) **Detail two points you would need to consider to ensure the investigation was a fair test.**

1 mark

1 mark

i) ....

ii) ....

2 Living Things

a) Suggest an investigation to test what snails prefer to eat.

....

....

....

1 mark

b) What would you keep the same during the experiment?

....

....

....

1 mark

c) What would you change during the experiment?

....

....

....

1 mark

3 Heading and Cooling

a) Some children investigated how food changes when it is heated and cooled.

They used a small candle to heat the food.

They put sand around the candle, to be safe.

Give **two** reasons why putting sand around the lighted candle made it safer.

i) .... 1 mark

ii) .... 1 mark

b) They used a thick cloth oven glove to hold the metal spoons and forks containing the food samples while they heated them.

Why was **thick cloth** a good material to wrap around the metal spoons when holding them above the candle flame?

....

....

1 mark

c) The children observed the way that each food changed when it was heated. They wrote down their results in a table.

Complete the table to say whether the changes were reversible or not.

Food	Change when heated	Is the change reversible?
peanut	singes and burns	no
butter	melts	
egg yolk	goes pale and hard	
flour	goes brown	

1 mark

4 Shadows

a) Helen has dropped her watch behind the sofa. It is dark behind the sofa, even though the lamp is on.

Explain why there is a shadow behind the sofa.

....

1 mark

b) Helen uses a mirror to shine light from the light bulb onto the watch.

What is the name of this process?

....

1 mark

c) On this diagram, draw a ray of light from the lightbulb to the watch. On the ray, draw an arrow to show which way the light travels.

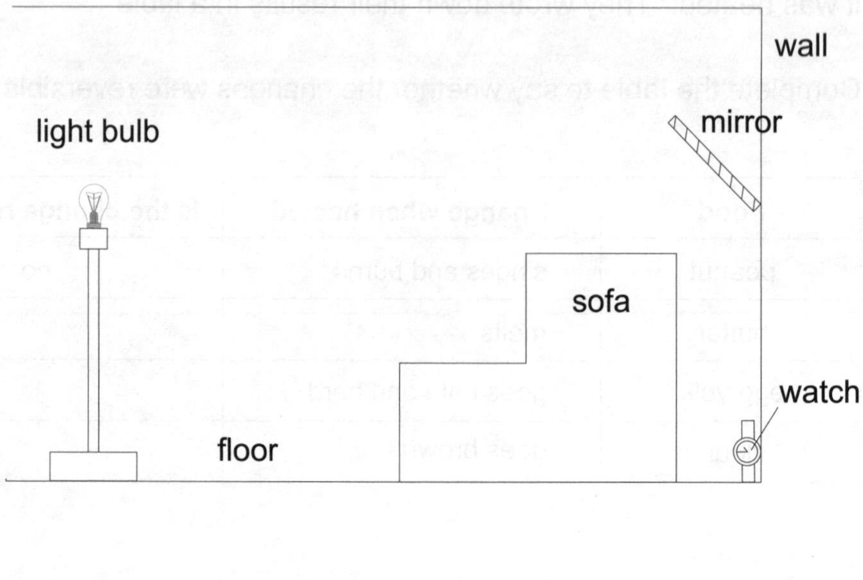

2 marks

5 The Water Cycle

a) Some children are learning about the water cycle.

Choose the correct word from below to fill in each of these sentences.

solid liquid gas

Rain is a ....

Water vapour is a ....

Snow is a ....

2 marks

b) The statements below describe the water cycle.
They are not in the correct order.

Write a number 1-5 in each box to show the correct order of the events in the water cycle.

One has been done for you.

☐ Clouds cool and water droplets form.

☐ Water vapour rises from the sea into the air.

☐ Droplets of water fall to the ground as rain.

1 The water flows in rivers to the sea.

☐ Water vapour cools and turns into water, which forms clouds.

1 mark

c) **What is the name of the process where water vapour rises from the sea into the air?**

....

1 mark

6 Plants

a) Jared and Rebecca are looking at plants.

This is a picture of a rose bush.

Write down two things from its surroundings that help the rose bush to grow.

i) ....

1 mark

ii) ....

1 mark

b) Jared says that the stem helps hold the plant up.

Describe one other thing that the stem does for the plant.

.... 1 mark

c) **Explain how leaves help the plant to grow well.**

....

.... 1 mark

This plant is eaten by aphids.

d) **Which of these words describes the aphids?**

Tick one box.

☐ producer

☐ consumer

☐ predator

1 mark

7 Forces

a) Jessica, Nigella and Scarlet are investigating forces. They want to find out how much force is needed to make a wooden box start to move.

They put the wooden box on a square of carpet on the table, and use string to tie on a container. Then they put weights in the container.

The weights pull down on the container.

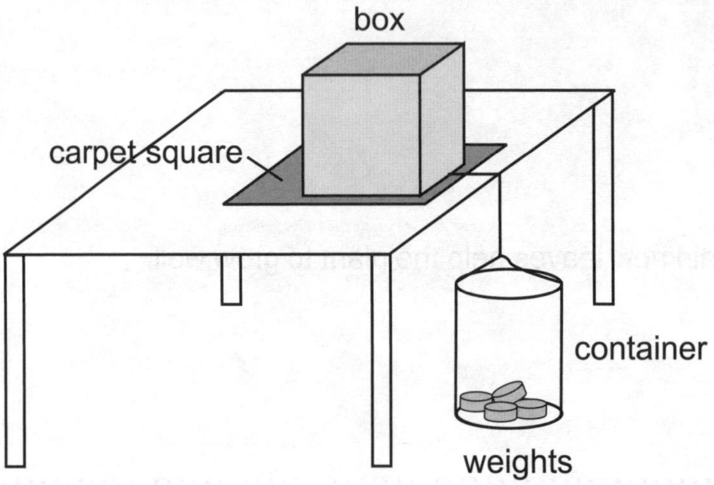

What is the name of the force pulling the container with the weights down?

....

1 mark

b) Jessica puts five weights in the container. The weights all weigh the same. The wooden box does not start to move.

What is the name of the force stopping the wooden box from moving?

....

1 mark

Jessica carries on putting weights in the container, until the wooden box starts to move. Nigella and Scarlet take out the weights and count them.

The children try the test again with a square of cardboard instead of a square of carpet, and again with a sheet of paper. They record their results in a table.

Surface	**Number of weights needed to get box moving**
Carpet	35
Cardboard	16
Paper	7

c) Write the name of the surface that the box moved over most easily.

....

1 mark

d) Why must they make sure that they use the same box each time?

....

1 mark

8 **Piglets**

The children go to visit a farm. One of the pigs has recently given birth to some piglets.

They ask the farmer what has happened to the pigs since they were born. They note down what he says.

2nd May	*Seven piglets were born*
18th May	*The piglets weighed twice as much as they did when they were born.*
4th June	*The piglets have stopped suckling from their mother, and now eat solid food.*

a) Write down the evidence that shows that the piglets grow after they are born.

....

....

1 mark

b) **Tick three things that all animals do.**

- ☐ feed
- ☐ wash
- ☐ roll in mud
- ☐ reproduce
- ☐ grow
- ☐ oink

3 marks

c) The children found some information about pregnancy in different animals.

animal	number of young it gives birth to	mass of each baby at birth	length of pregnancy
pig	6	1kg	114 days
mouse	10	1g	20 days
cat	4	100g	60 days
goat	2	3.5 kg	150 days

Describe the relationship between the length of the pregnancy and the size of the baby when it is born.

....

....

2 marks

9 Electricity

a) Geoffrey makes a circuit with some wire, a battery and a bulb.

He puts a switch in his circuit

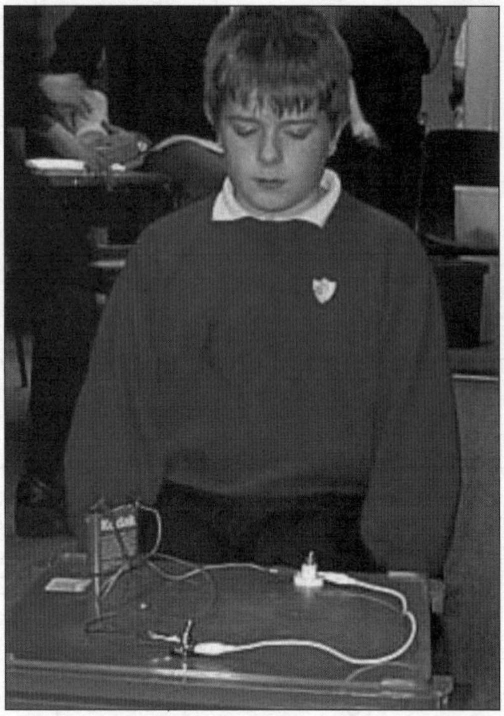

In this picture, the switch is open (off), and the light bulb is not glowing.

Draw a **diagram** of Geoffrey's circuit with the switch open.

Include these symbols.

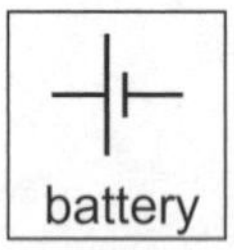

1 mark

b) Geoffrey closes the switch. The light bulb starts glowing.

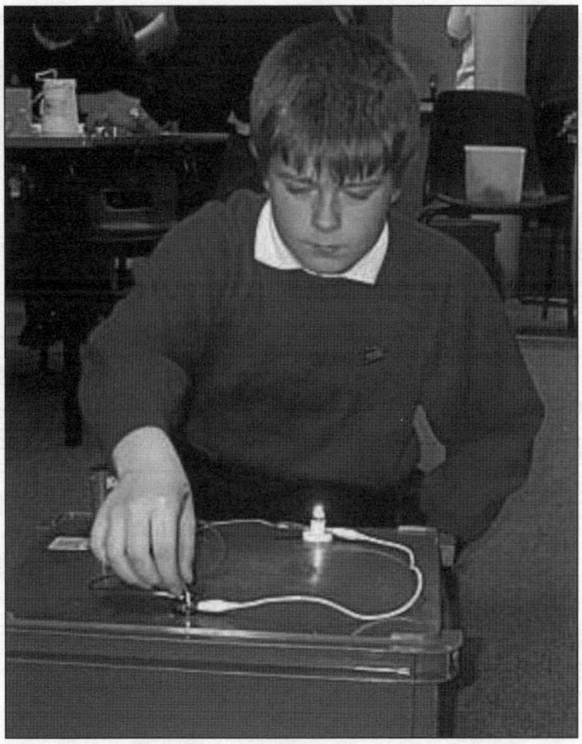

Why can the electricity make the bulb glow when the switch is closed?

....

1 mark

c) Geoffrey wants to make the bulb shine **more brightly.**

Which of the following things should he do to his circuit?

Tick **ONE** box.

Add more bulbs ☐

Add more wire ☐

Add another battery ☐

1 mark

10 Dissolving

Shauna is using salt to investigate dissolving.

She has three different types of salt:

coarse

medium

fine

a) Shauna dissolves 20 g of each type of salt in 100 cm^3 of water.
She measures how long the salt takes to completely dissolve.

She stirs each container with the **same** spoon, at the **same** speed.

Type of salt	Time it took to dissolve (seconds)		
Coarse	280	270	274
Medium	121	133	127
Fine	50	58	60

Which type of salt dissolved the fastest?

....

1 mark

b) Shauna did her test more than once.

Explain why Shauna did the test more than once.

....

....

1 mark

c) How did the size of the grains of salt affect the time taken for them to dissolve?

....

....

2 marks

shp21 1b

SCIENCE
KEY STAGE 2

Practice Paper 2
Test B

45 MINUTES

TOTAL SCORE

FIRST GO:	
SECOND GO:	
THIRD GO:	

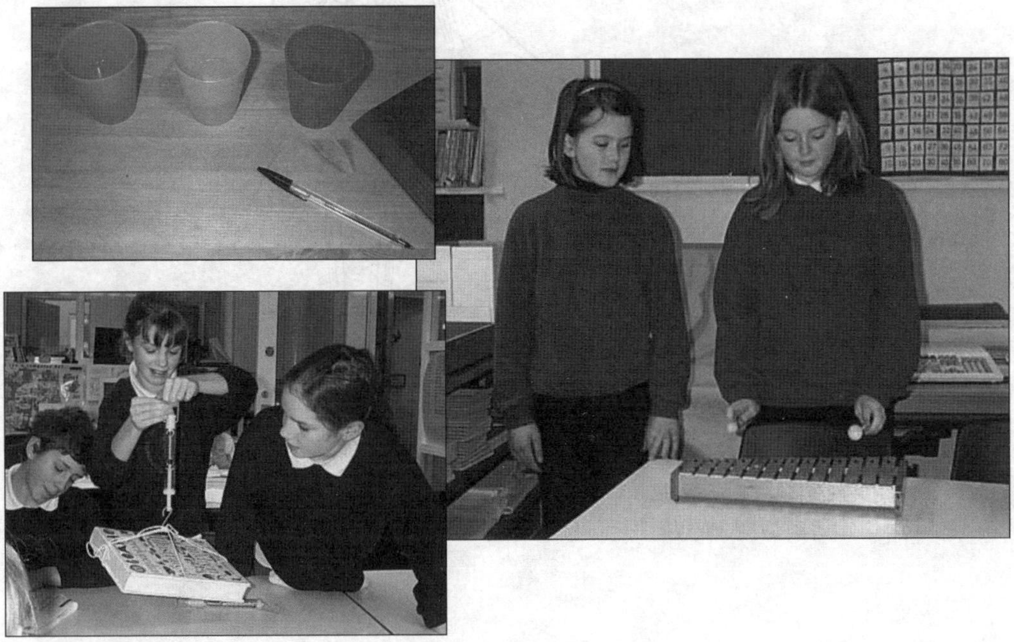

FIRST NAME	
LAST NAME	
SCHOOL	

1 The Skeleton

a) This is a drawing of a human skeleton.

Label the parts of the skeleton.

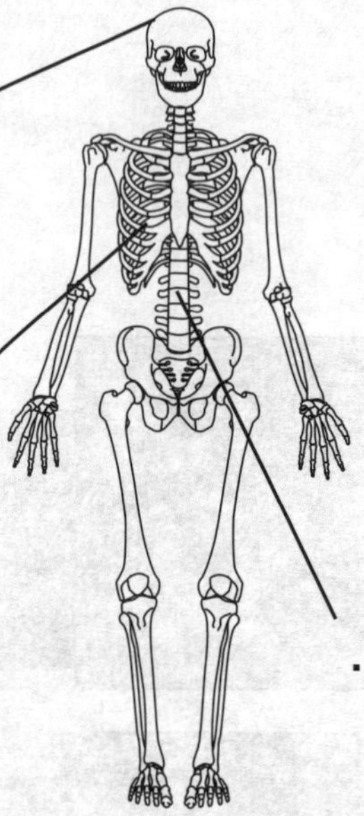

skull.

ribs

backbone.

2 marks

b) **Describe TWO ways that the skeleton is important to the body.**

(i) keeps you stable.

1 mark

(ii) Keeps muscles in place.

1 mark

c) The length of the human foot changes throughout a person's life cycle.

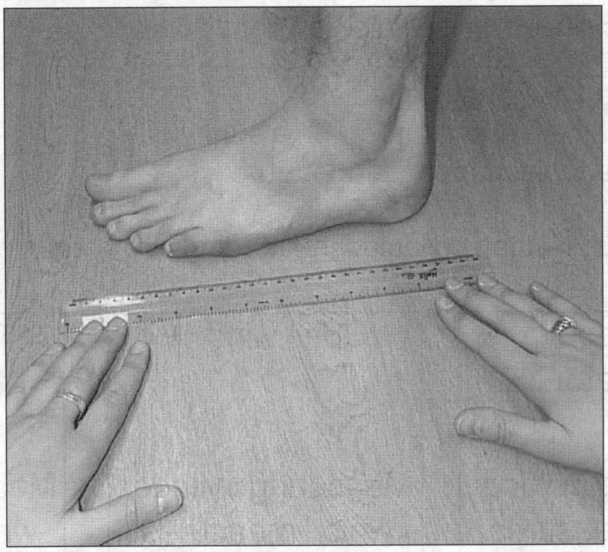

These boxes show the length of one person's foot at different stages of their life.

Draw lines to match each length of foot to the correct stage of life.

One has been done for you.

8 cm	child
17 cm	adult
30 cm	baby
25 cm	teenager

1 mark

2 Solids and Water

Nathan wanted to establish which conditions yeast grows best in.
He placed the same amount of yeast and sugar in 3 measuring cylinders.
He put the cylinders in the following conditions.

- On a shelf above a radiator
- Next to an open window on a sunny day
- On a table at room temperature

After an hour, Nathan collected the readings from each of the cylinders.

Shelf above radiator	Open window	Table at room temperature
Measuring cylinder which measures	Measuring cylinder which measures	Measuring cylinder which measures
837 ml	615 ml	510 ml

a) The yeast grew best in which location?

....

1 mark

b) What was the cylinder reading at the location from part a)?

....

1 mark

c) What do these results tell us about micro-organisms?

....

1 mark

d) Name 2 ways of preventing the spread of micro-organisms.

i) .... ii) ....

2 marks

3 Sound

A group of children wanted to find out which material is best for muffling sound. They tried the following materials:

Polythene
Foam padding
Stone
Cotton sheet

a) Which material do you think would be best for muffling sound?

....

1 mark

b) Why do you think that?

....

....

1 mark

c) Explain how sound travels.

....

....

1 mark

4 **Solids and Liquids**

a) Charlie and Mark put three ice cubes in a glass.

What is the name for the **process** when a solid turns into a liquid?

....

1 mark

b) They saw tiny drops of liquid forming on the outside of the glass.

Where did the liquid on the outside of the glass come from?

....

1 mark

c) Charlie and Mark put three more ice cubes into another glass.

They wrap this glass in a towel.

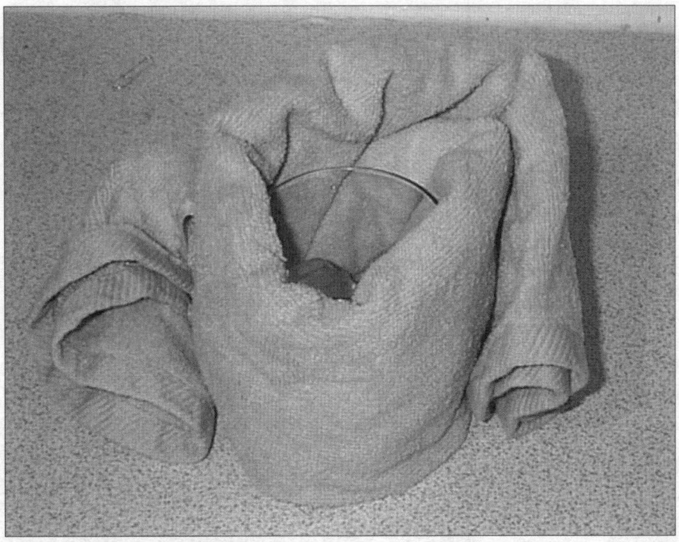

What effect would the towel have on the ice cubes in the second glass?

Tick **ONE** box.

The ice cubes in the second glass would:

turn to liquid in the same time ☐

turn to liquid more slowly ☐

not turn to liquid at all ☐

turn to liquid more quickly ☐

☐ 1 mark

5

Life Cycle of a Plant

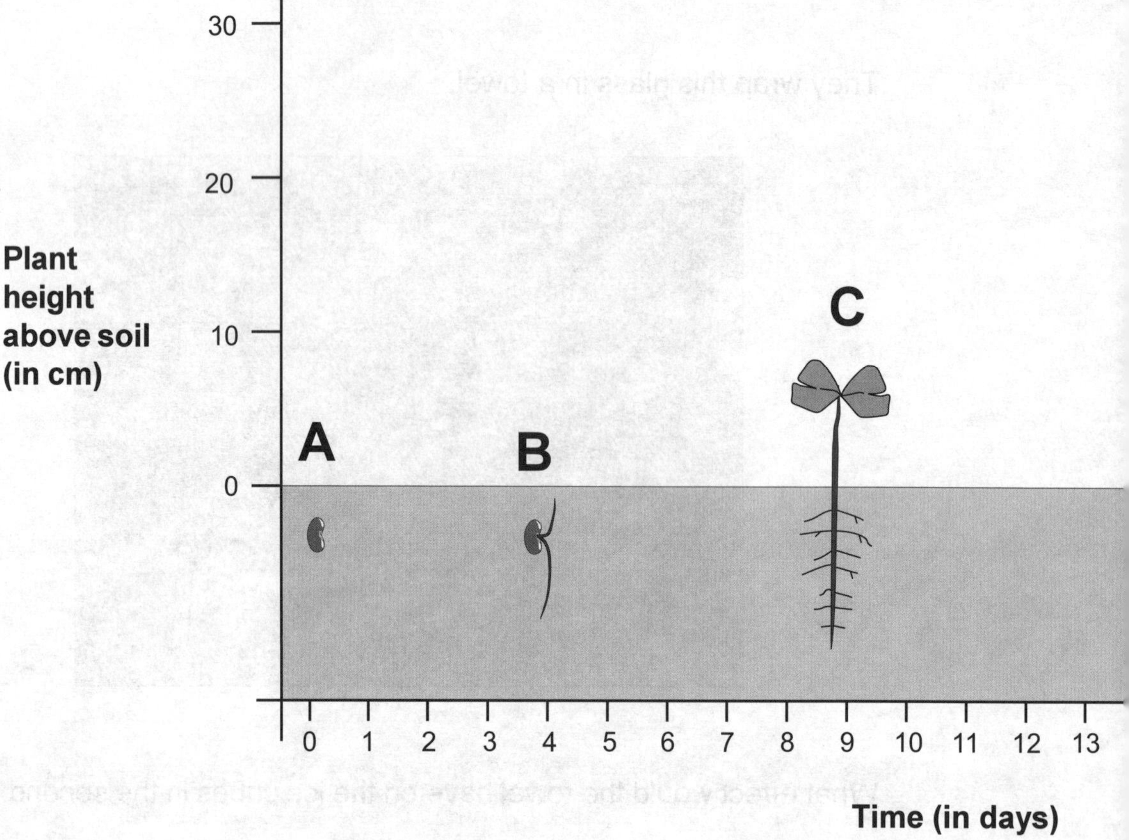

a) Class 6K planted seeds of a fast growing plant.

How tall did this plant grow above the soil in 16 days?

....

1 mark

b) How many days did the total life cycle take?

....

1 mark

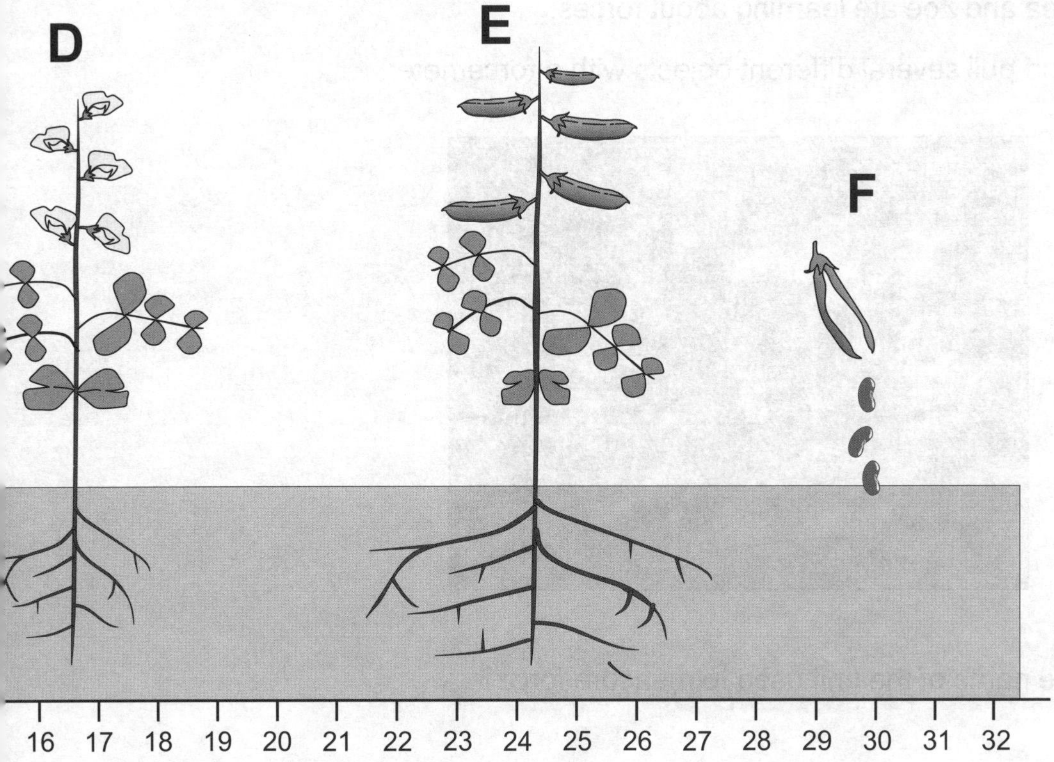

c) The diagram shows the stages in the plant's life cycle.
They are labelled A-F.

Write the correct letter for each stage in the table.

Stage	Letter from diagram
fruits on plant	
pollination	
seed dispersal	
germination	

2 marks

d) What do these parts do to help the plant grow well?

i) Leaves...

....

1 mark

ii) Roots...

....

1 mark

6 **Forces**

Chloë, Thea and Zoë are learning about forces.

They lift and pull several different objects with a forcemeter.

a) What is the name of the unit used to measure force?

1 mark

....

b) Thea writes the results in a table.

Action	Force needed to make it start moving
Lifting a brick	25
Lifting a book	8
Lifting a pencil case	4
Pulling a boot across the desk	12

Look at the table. Which object was hardest to move?

1 mark

....

c) When Chloë lifts the book, she is pulling it up.

What is the name of the force pulling the book down?

....

1 mark

d) Thea pulls a boot across different kinds of floor.

She finds it harder to pull the boot on the carpet than on the tiled floor.

What is the name of the force that increases when Thea pulls the boot on the carpet?

....

1 mark

7 **The Earth**

Jolene and Sid are using different-sized balls to model the Sun and the Earth.

The Earth goes round the Sun.

a) Describe **ONE** other way that the Earth moves in space.

....

1 mark

b) How long does it take the Earth to revolve around the Sun for one complete turn?

Tick **ONE** box.

1 day ☐ 1 month ☐

1 year ☐ 6 months ☐

1 mark

c) Jolene uses a globe as a model of the Earth. She uses a torch as a model of the Sun. The arrows in this picture show the way that Jolene turns the model of the Earth.

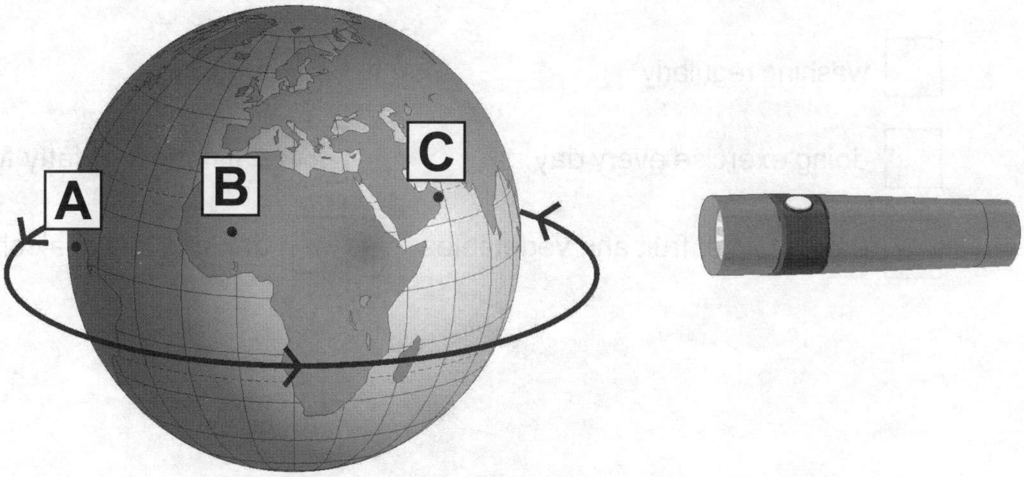

When the model Earth is in the position shown in the picture, what times of day are shown at points **A**, **B** and **C** on the globe?

Choose one of the words below to complete each sentence.
You may only use each word **once**.

sunrise **night-time** **afternoon**

sunset **morning**

One of them has been done for you.

At **A** it is night-time

At **B** it is ....

At **C** it is ....

1 mark

1 mark

8 The Heart

a) **Which of these activities could lead to a smaller chance of heart disease?**

Tick **TWO** of the boxes.

☐ washing regularly
☐ smoking
☐ doing exercise every day
☐ eating lots of fatty foods
☐ eating lots of fruit and vegetables
☐ drinking lots of alcohol

2 marks

b) This is a picture of the human heart.

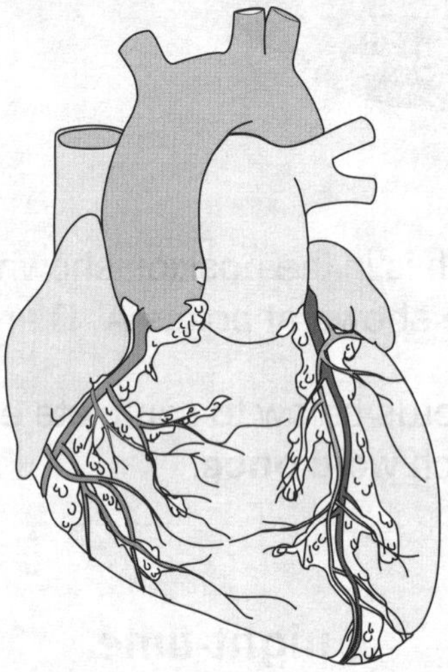

What does the heart do inside the body?

....

....

1 mark

c) What is the name of the blood vessels which carry blood **away** from the heart?

....

1 mark

d) Joanne took part in three different activities. She measured her heart rate straight away after each activity. She measured her heart rate again after she had rested for 30 minutes. She recorded her results in a table.

Complete the table to show her heart rate after resting for 30 minutes.

Activity	**Heart Rate**	
	just after activity	after resting for 30 minutes
reading	73	72
playing tennis	167	....
jogging	135	....

1 mark

e) **Explain how you decided what heart rates to write in the table.**

....

....

1 mark

9 **Evaporation**

Some children carried out a fair test on evaporation. They used three identical containers with 100 cm^3 water in each one. They put each container in a different room. Each room was at a different temperature.

Room A	15 °C
Room B	20 °C
Room C	11 °C

a) The children used the same volume of water in each container, to make the test a fair test. Name one other thing they did to make the test a fair test.

1 mark

b) The children measured the volume of water in each container after five days.

Write A, B or C under each bar in this chart, to show which rooms the containers of water were in.

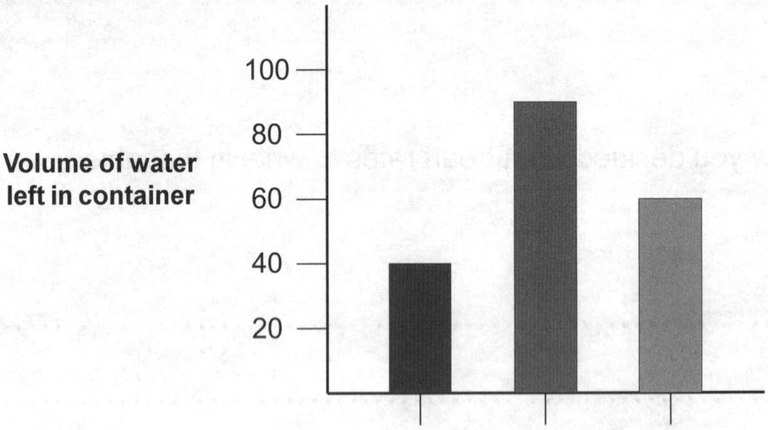

1 mark

c) Describe how the volume of water left depends on the temperature of the room.

2 marks

shp21 2b

SCIENCE
KEY STAGE 2

Practice Paper 3
Test A

45 MINUTES

TOTAL SCORE

FIRST GO: ____

SECOND GO: ____

THIRD GO: ____

FIRST NAME	
LAST NAME	
SCHOOL	

CGP

1 ***Smoking and Health***

a) This graph shows how the number of adults smoking **changed** between 1980 and 1990.

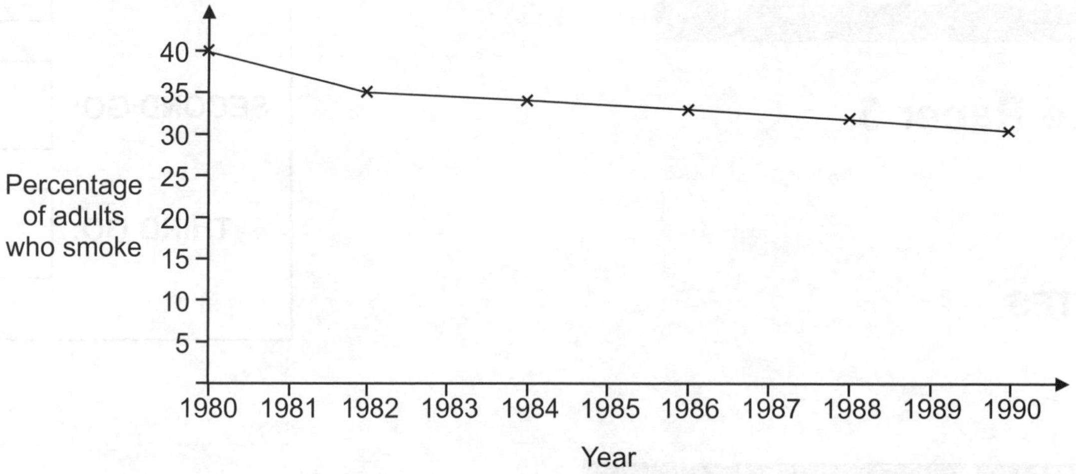

Look at the graph and answer these questions.

(i) Describe how the number of people smoking **changed** between 1980 and 1990.

....

....

1 mark

(ii) Give ONE possible reason for this change.

....

....

1 mark

b) David and Laura asked four adults some questions to find out whether or not they had a healthy lifestyle.

This table shows how the adults replied.

Name	Takes regular exercise	Has healthy diet	Smokes
Rita	Yes	Yes	Yes
Sunil	Yes	Yes	No
Erica	No	No	Yes
Alan	No	Yes	No

Which adult in the table has the least healthy lifestyle?

....

1 mark

c) Name one disease which you can get by smoking.

....

1 mark

2 Electricity

a) Kylie has made a circuit using two new batteries, a new bulb, and a switch.

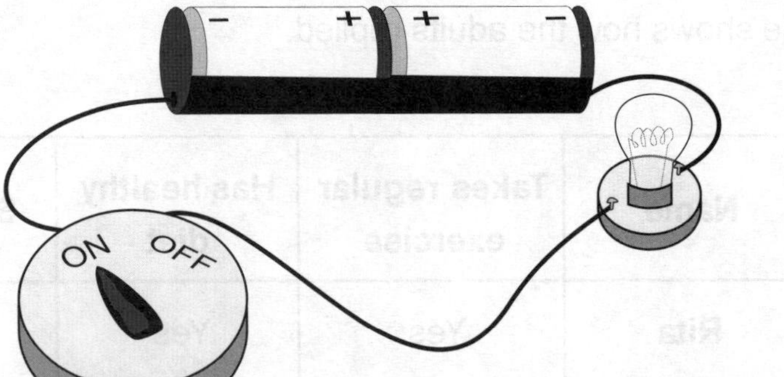

Why is the bulb in this circuit not lit up?

....

1 mark

b) Draw a circuit diagram of Kylie's circuit.

Use these symbols.

1 mark

3 Properties

Jacob and Lucy are investigating the materials from which some classroom equipment is made.

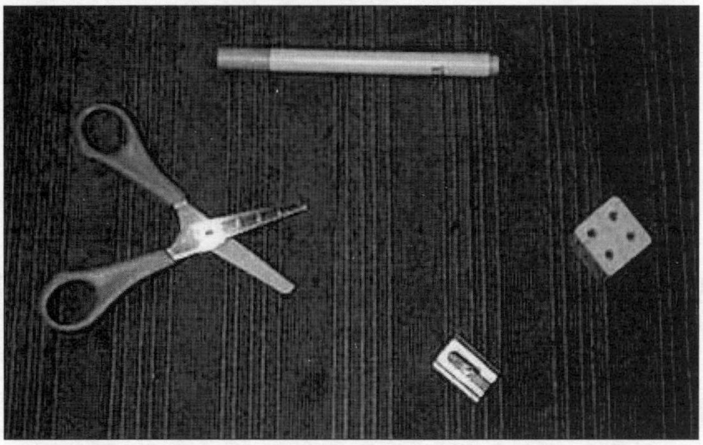

They do some tests on a pair of scissors, a die, a felt-tipped pen and a pencil sharpener, and make a table to show the results.

Fill in the gaps in this table.

	Pen	Scissors	Pencil sharpener	Die
Made of:	plastic	plastic and steel	steel	wood
Does it float?	yes		no	
Is it attracted by a magnet?		plastic - no steel - yes	yes	

4 marks

4 The Solar System

a) Nathan was to make a model solar system incorporating the Earth, Sun and Moon. In his fruit bowl he has a water melon, an orange and a grape. Using size as a guide, which fruit should he use to represent the Earth, Sun and Moon. Connect the words by drawing a line between them.

Earth	**grape**
Sun	**orange**
Moon	**water melon**

1 mark

Nathan asked two friends to help him model the movement of the Earth, Sun and Moon in the solar system.

b) Describe the movement of the Moon in the solar system.

....

....

1 mark

c) Describe the movement of the Earth in the solar system.

....

....

1 mark

d) On a clear day in June, Aiden notices that his shadow is long and pointing in a westerly direction. Approximately what time of day do you think it could be?

i) 12 noon ☐ ii) 8 am ☐ iii) 7 pm ☐ iv) 2 pm ☐

1 mark

e) Explain your answer.

....

....

1 mark

f) How was the shadow formed?

....

....

1 mark

5 Sound

a) Jack stretches an elastic band around an empty plastic food box.
He pulls on the elastic band and lets go. It makes a sound.

What is happening to the elastic band when it is making a sound?

....

1 mark

b) Jack pulls harder on the elastic band before letting go.

Describe how this changes the sound made by the elastic band.

....

1 mark

c) Jack takes the elastic band off the box.
He replaces it with a longer one.

What effect does the length of the rubber band have on the sound it makes when Jack pulls and lets go?

....

....

2 marks

6 Separating Mixtures

a) Anna and Neil have some water in a bucket that they have scooped out of the sea.

The water has salt, sand, small stones and pieces of seaweed mixed into it.

The children want to separate all the different bits out of the water.

Which method should they use first to separate the pieces of stone and seaweed from the mixture?

Tick **ONE** box.

condensing	☐	evaporating	☐
filtering	☐	sieving	☐

1 mark

b) Which method should they use next to separate the sand from the mixture?

Tick **ONE** box.

condensing ☐ evaporating ☐

filtering ☐ sieving ☐

1 mark

c) The water left in the bucket is nearly clear now.
The children can't see the individual grains of salt.

Why is this? Explain what has happened to the salt.

....

1 mark

d) The separated salty water is poured into a pan and gently heated until a browny-white solid is all that is left.

What has happened to the water?

....

1 mark

e) If the heat under the pan was hotter, would it take more or less time to dry up? Explain why this is.

....

....

2 marks

7 Green Plants

a) Bill and Hillary sowed some grass seeds on a piece of ground behind their school.

Name **ONE** thing all seeds **must** have to **start** to grow.

1 mark

....

b) When the grass has grown the children decide to do an experiment on it.

Bill covers a patch of grass with a black plastic sheet and Hillary covers another patch with a clear plastic sheet.

After five days what would the grass look like under Bill's sheet of black plastic?

Tick **ONE** box.

completely dead	☐	healthy and green	☐
yellow	☐	very dark green	☐

1 mark

c) After 5 days what is the grass under Hillary's clear plastic sheet likely to look like?

....

....

1 mark

d) Green plants need light to grow and be healthy.

Name **TWO** other things green plants need to grow healthily.

....

....

2 marks

8 Forces

a) Samantha did some experiments using a forcemeter.

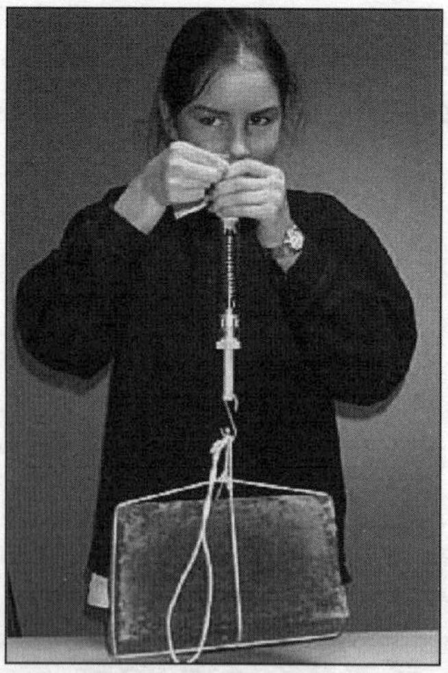

She hung different objects from the forcemeter and measured their weight in newtons.

What is the name of the force the forcemeter is measuring in this picture?

Tick **ONE** box.

magnetism ☐ water upthrust ☐

gravity ☐ hot air currents ☐

1 mark

b) Samantha noticed there was a spring inside the forcemeter.

Why does a forcemeter contain a spring?

Tick ONE box.

Because the spring is:

clever ☐ bendy ☐

stretchy ☐ strong ☐

1 mark

c) Samantha recorded her results.

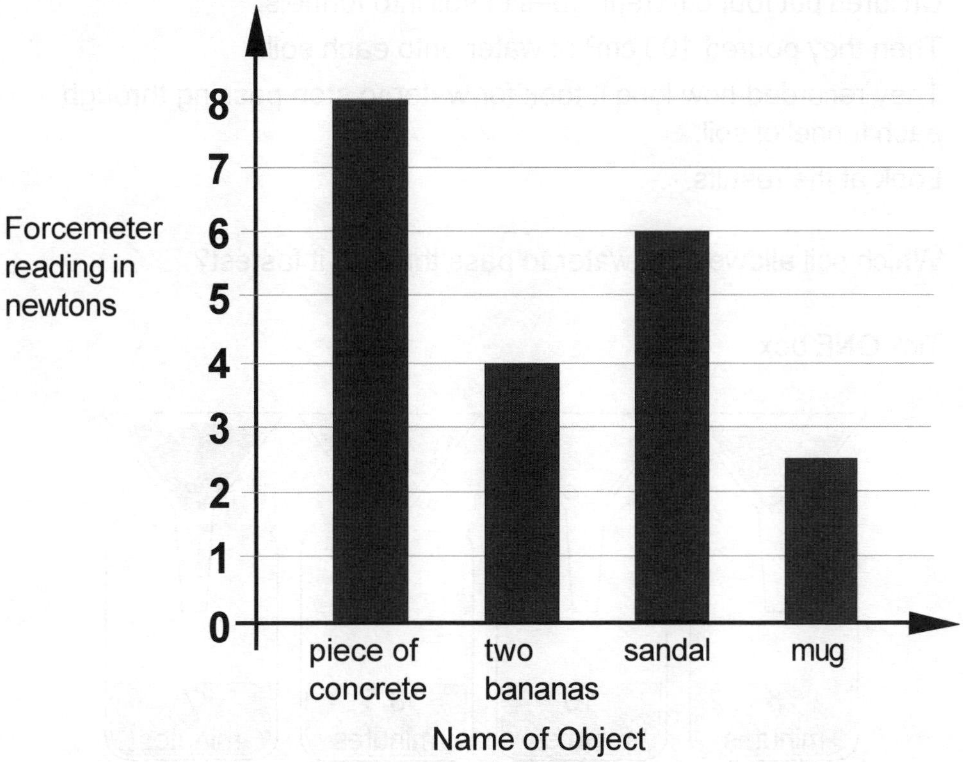

What was the reading on the forcemeter when the sandal was hung from it?

....

1 mark

d) If the same sandal was hung on a forcemeter underwater would it still have the same weight in newtons?

Explain why this is.

....

....

1 mark

9 Soil

a) Children put four different types of soil into funnels.

Then they poured 100 cm^3 of water onto each soil.

They recorded how long it took for water to stop passing through each funnel of soil.

Look at the results.

Which soil allowed the water to pass through it fastest?

Tick **ONE** box.

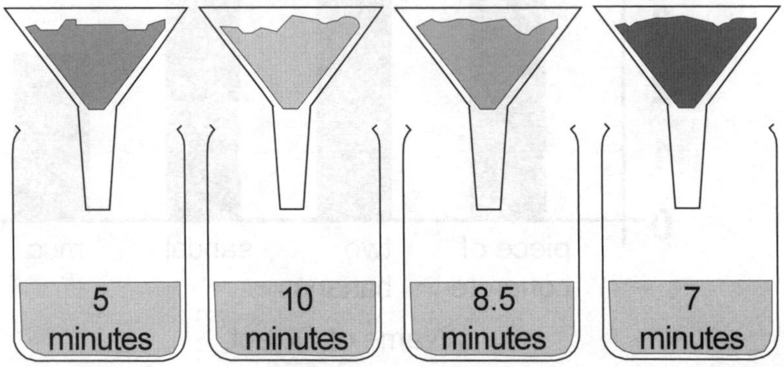

A	B	C	D
☐	☐	☐	☐

1 mark

b) Sand has quite large particles which let water through easily.

Clay has smaller particles and does not let water through as easily.

The table shows the four types of soil that were tested.

Which funnel contained which soil?

Write the letter for each funnel to complete this table.

soil	funnel
all clay	....
mostly clay, some sand	....
mostly sand, some clay	....
all sand	....

1 mark

c) The children tried pouring 100 cm^3 of water over small stones in a funnel.

They wanted to know how the stones compare with the different types of soil.

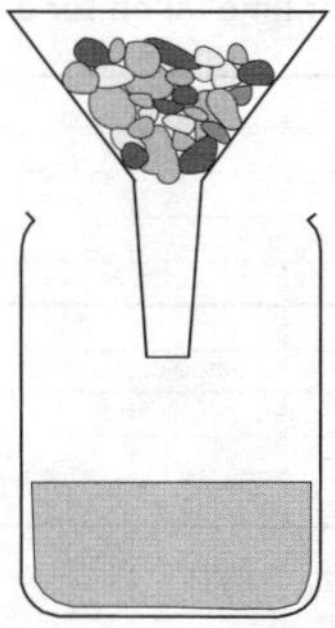

Put the types of soil and small stones in order of which allowed the water to pass through fastest.

Write the letters in the correct boxes in the table.

A soil type A
B soil type B
C soil type C
D soil type D
E small stones

Speed	Soil Type
fastest	
2nd fastest	
3rd fastest	
4th fastest	
slowest	

1 mark

10

Gravity

Bethan carried out an experiment to test how spinners weighted with paper clips fall when dropped.

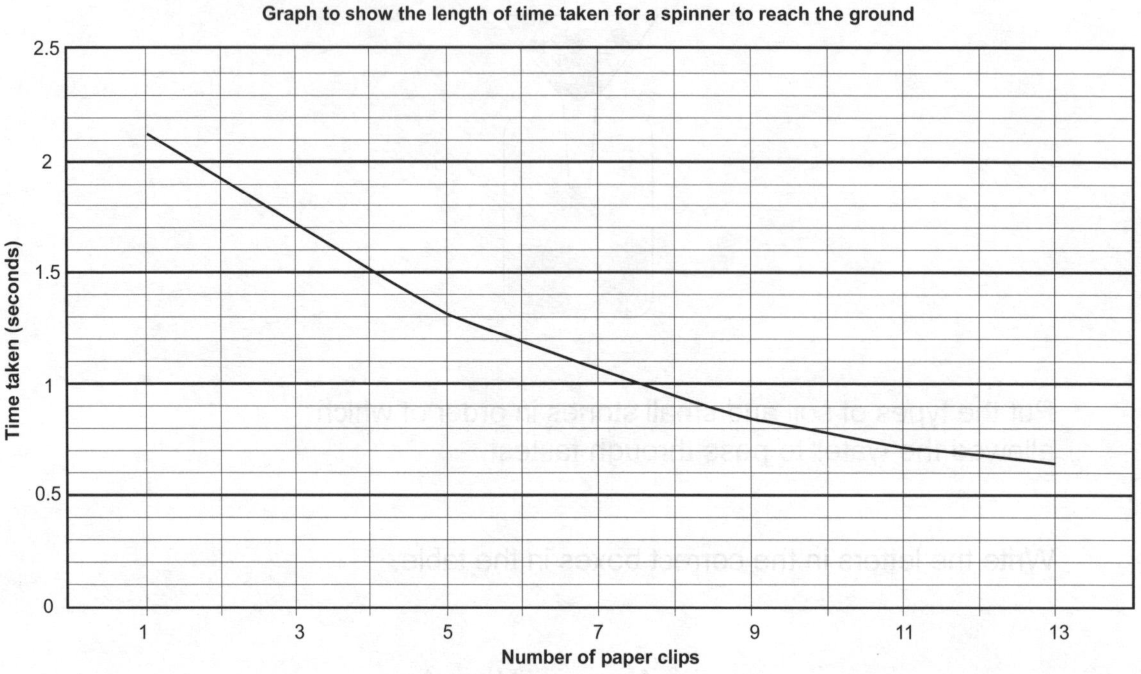

a) How long did it take the spinner to reach the ground when 8 paper clips were used?

....

1 mark

b) What is the relationship between the time taken to reach the ground and the number of paper clips used? Use the graph to help explain your answer.

....

....

1 mark

shp21 3a

1102

SCIENCE
KEY STAGE 2

Practice Paper 3
Test B

45 MINUTES

TOTAL SCORE

FIRST GO:

SECOND GO:

THIRD GO:

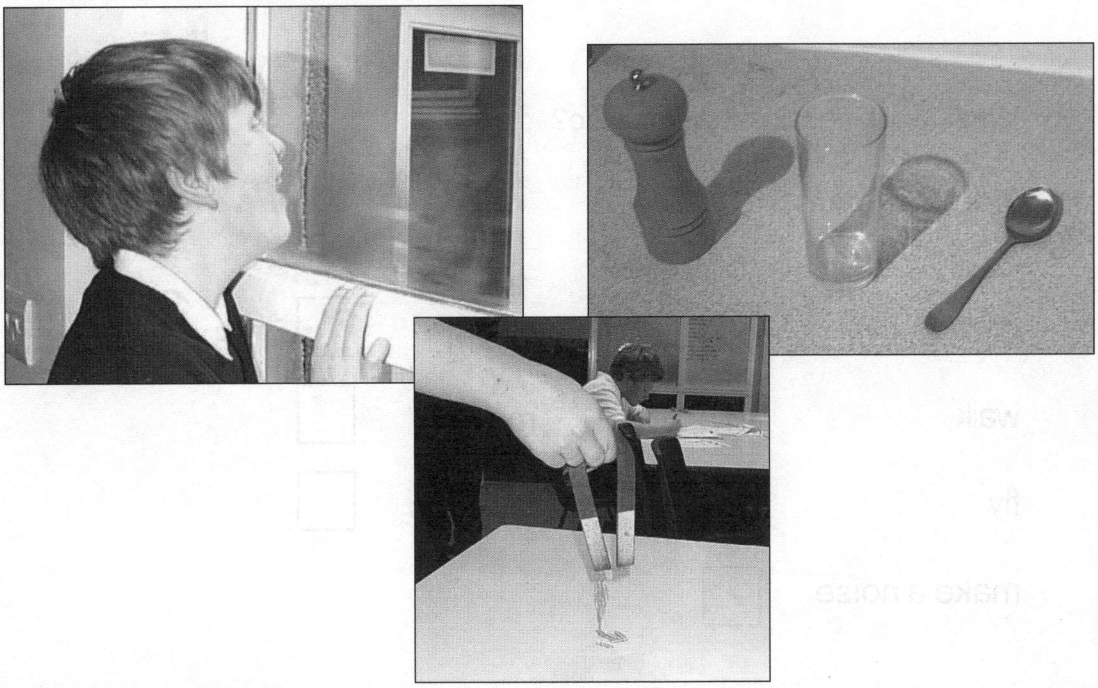

FIRST NAME	
LAST NAME	
SCHOOL	

CGP

1 Woodland

Some children studied the animals in a small area of woodland.

This is a picture of a barn owl.

a) What two things do all animals do?

Tick **TWO** boxes.

grow	☐	sing	☐
walk	☐	move	☐
fly	☐	lay eggs	☐
make a noise	☐		

2 marks

b) The barn owl hunts small animals such as mice and voles.
It has sharp claws and a sharp beak to help it catch them.

Describe one more way that the barn owl is adapted to hunting small animals.

....

....

1 mark

c) These pictures show what some of the animals in the woodland eat.

gall wasp eats oak tree

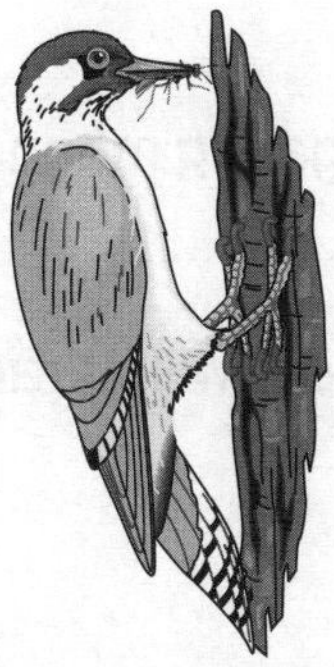

woodpecker eats gall wasp

owl eats vole

Use the information in the pictures.

Write the names of three living things to show one food chain in this woodland.

.... → .... → ....

1 mark

d) **Choose words to fill in these sentences about the living things in the woodland.**

producer   predator   prey   mammal   plant

One is done for you.

The oak tree is a **producer**

The gall wasp is ....

1 mark

The woodpecker is a ....

1 mark

2 Magnets

a) Some children are investigating magnets.

Say whether these magnets will attract or repel.

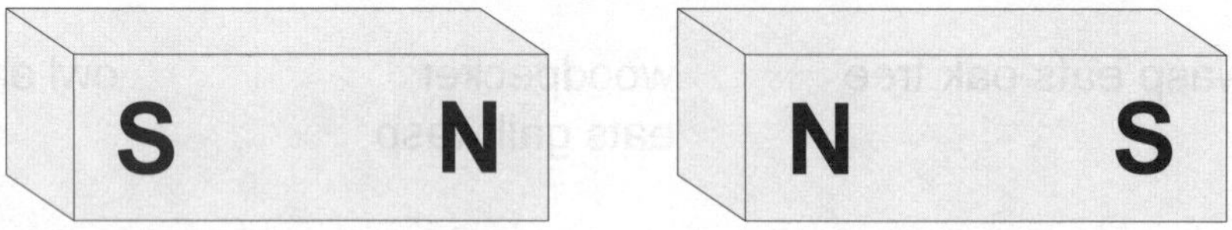

1 mark

The magnets will ....

b) The children have some metal paperclips and some plastic ones.

The magnet only attracts the metal paperclips.

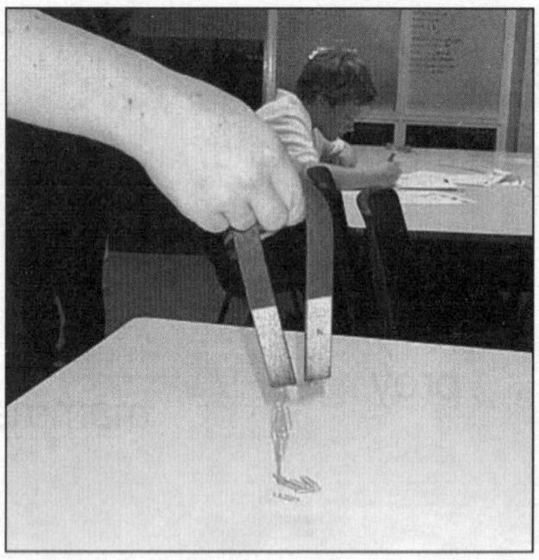

Say why the magnet does not attract the plastic paperclips.

....

....

1 mark

c) The children find out how many paperclips they can pick up at once.

They try with one magnet, then two magnets, then three, then four.

They put their results into a table.

Fill in the gap in the table to show how many paperclips you think three magnets together would have picked up.

Number of magnets	Number of paperclips picked up
1	12
2	23
3	....
4	45

1 mark

d) **What do you think the children did to make sure their test was a fair one?**

Tick **TWO** boxes.

They made sure that all the magnets were identical. ☐

They made sure that all the paperclips were the same size. ☐

They did the test in the afternoon. ☐

They recorded their results straight away. ☐

2 marks

3 Yeast and Bread

a) David has been baking bread. He made some dough with flour, water, sugar and yeast. He left the dough in a warm place for half an hour.

After half an hour, the dough had **risen**.
There were lots of tiny **bubbles** in it.

Tick **ONE** box to say where the bubbles had come from.

☐ The yeast produces gas as it grows.

☐ The dough is breathing.

☐ The bubbles were in the water to start with.

1 mark

b) David decided to do an investigation to see what bread dough needed in order to rise properly. He wanted to find out if it needed **sugar** and **warmth**.

David needs to use **four** bowls of dough — one **cold with sugar**, one **cold without sugar**, one **warm with sugar** and one **warm without sugar**.

Explain why David needs to use **four** bowls of dough.

....

....

2 marks

c) David put his results in a table.

Dough	Did it rise?
Warm with sugar	Yes
Cold with sugar	No
Warm without sugar	No
Cold without sugar	No

What **two** things does dough need to rise?

.... and ....

1 mark

4 Breathing

When Cuthbert breathes onto the window, it becomes misty.

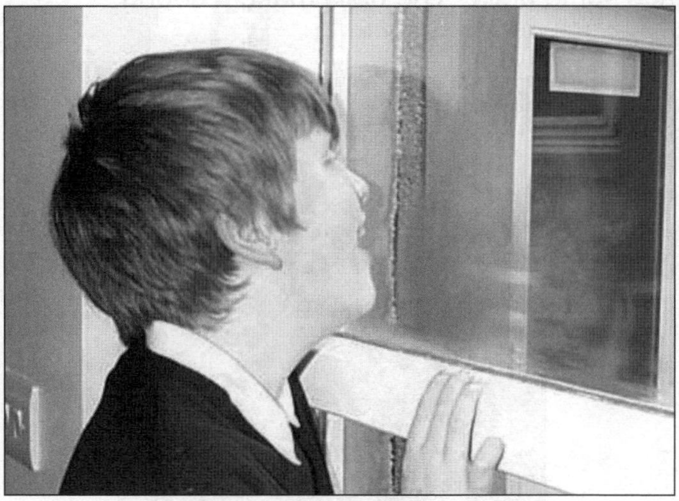

a) Name the process that causes the window to become misty.

....

1 mark

b) Why does the window become misty when Cuthbert breathes on it?

Tick one of the boxes.

☐ Cuthbert's breath is hotter than the window.

☐ Cuthbert's breath is colder than the window.

☐ The window is open.

1 mark

5 Sound

a) Jessica and Rachel are investigating sound.

Jessica rings some bells. The bells make a sound.

Describe how the bells make a sound.

....

1 mark

b) What does the sound travel through to reach Rachel's ears?

....

1 mark

Jessica rings the bells, then touches them on her jumper. They stop ringing.

c) Why do the bells stop making a sound?

....

1 mark

d) Rachel has a clock that ticks loudly. She wants to make it quieter.

She needs to find out what materials are good for stopping the sound of the clock from getting to her ears.

Rachel tries wrapping the clock in four different materials.

Each time, she finds out how many layers she needs before she can't hear the ticking any more.

Material	Number of layers
Paper	16
Cardboard	7
Cotton sheet	11
Wool blanket	6

Which material is the best at making the sound of the clock quieter?

....

1 mark

6 Looking at Flowering Plants

This is a picture of a plant that is pollinated by bees.

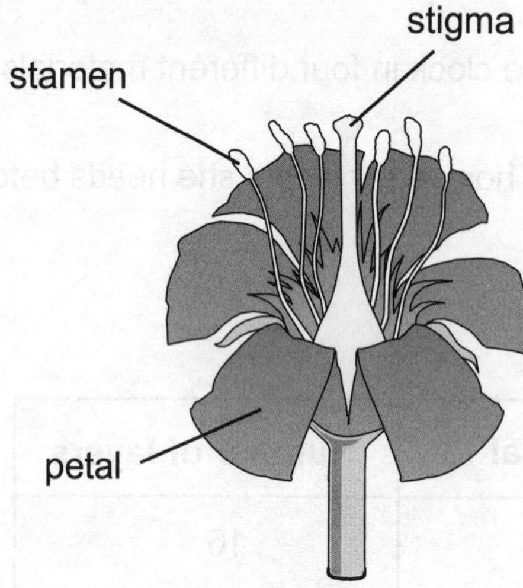

a) Which part of the plant collects pollen from bees?

....

1 mark

b) How do the petals help the plant to become pollinated?

....

....

1 mark

c) This plant is pollinated by bees.

Write down one other way that some other plants are pollinated.

....

1 mark

d) This is a key for some flowering plants.

Look at it very carefully. Use the key to answer the two questions below.

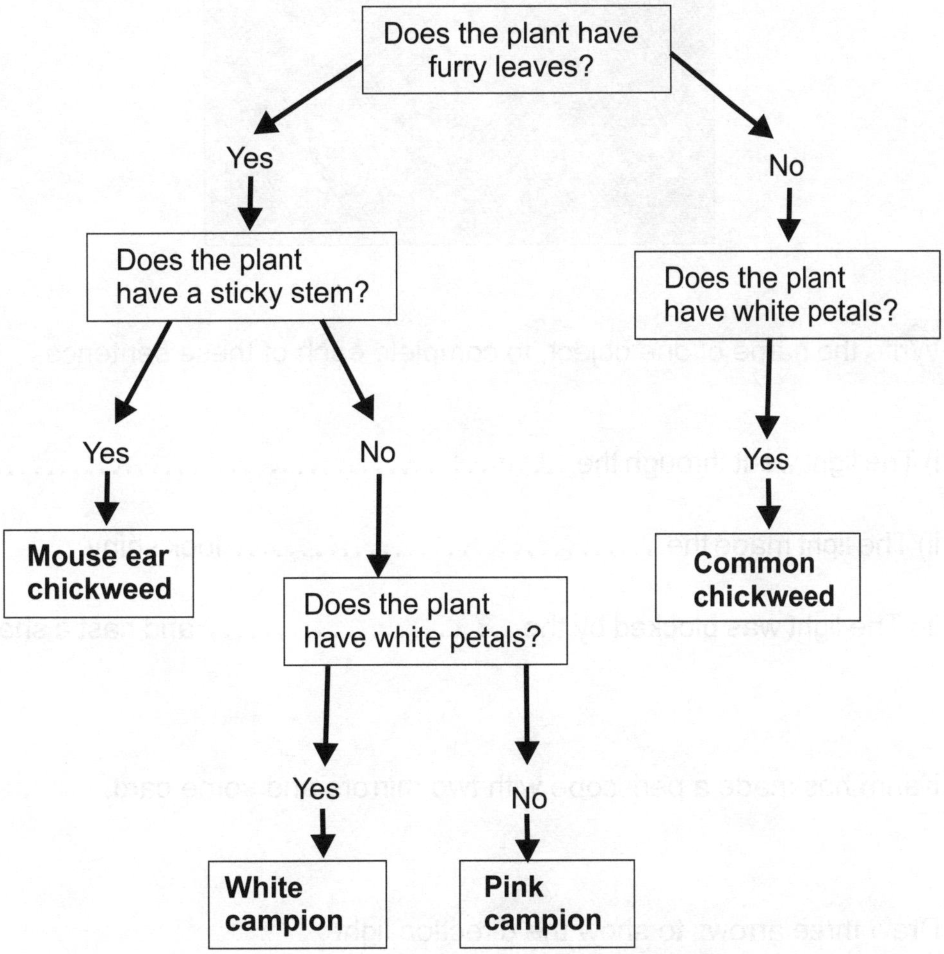

Which plant has white petals, a non-sticky stem and furry leaves?

....

1 mark

What colour petals does common chickweed have?

....

1 mark

7 Light

a) Karim shone a torch onto some objects from the kitchen.

Write the name of one object, to complete each of these sentences.

i) The light went through the ....

1 mark

ii) The light made the .... look shiny.

1 mark

iii) The light was blocked by the .... and cast a shadow.

1 mark

b) Karim has made a periscope with two mirrors and some card.

Draw three arrows to show the direction light travels to allow him to see over the wall.

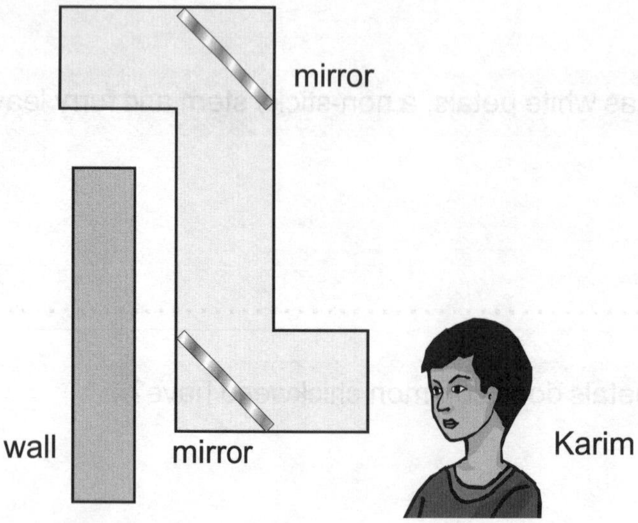

1 mark

8 Liquids and Gases

a) Bina placed a saucer of perfume on a table in a classroom. After a few seconds, Andrew claimed that he could smell it. How was Andrew able to smell the perfume when he was a few metres away from it?

....

.... 1 mark

b) Bina left the perfume on the table for a few days. The liquid seemed to 'disappear'. What happened to the liquid?

.... 1 mark

c) Name 2 factors which affect how quickly the perfume dries up.

1) .... 1 mark

2) .... 1 mark

9 **Electricity**

This is a diagram of the inside of Chantelle's doorbell.

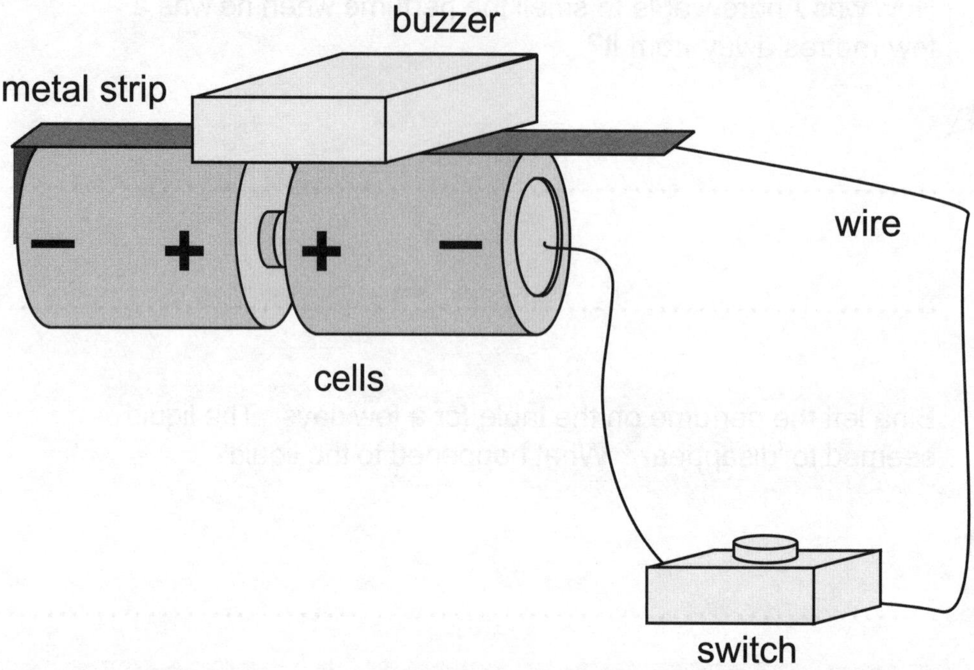

a) If Chantelle rings the doorbell, will it work?

....

1 mark

b) The cells and buzzer are connected by a metal strip.

What makes metal a good material to connect the cells and the buzzer?

....

....

1 mark

c) In the space below, draw a circuit diagram of Chantelle's doorbell with the cells put in correctly.

Use these symbols in your diagram.

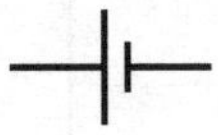

cell

buzzer

switch

1 mark

1 mark

10 Health

Peter was undecided about which breakfast cereal to choose. His Dad suggested that he chose the healthiest. Below is a table of the nutritional information on the cereal packets.

Breakfast cereal	Amount of sugar per 100g	Amount of fibre per 100g	Amount of protein per 100g
Rice Puffs	10g	1g	6g
Wheat Bites	5g	10g	11g
Frost Flakes	40g	2g	4g
Fruity Bran	22g	9g	8g
Bran cereal	22g	15g	10g

a) Which is the healthiest cereal?

....

1 mark

b) Explain why.

....

....

1 mark

shp21 3b

SCIENCE
KEY STAGE 2

Practice Paper 2
Test A

45 MINUTES

TOTAL SCORE

FIRST GO:

SECOND GO:

THIRD GO:

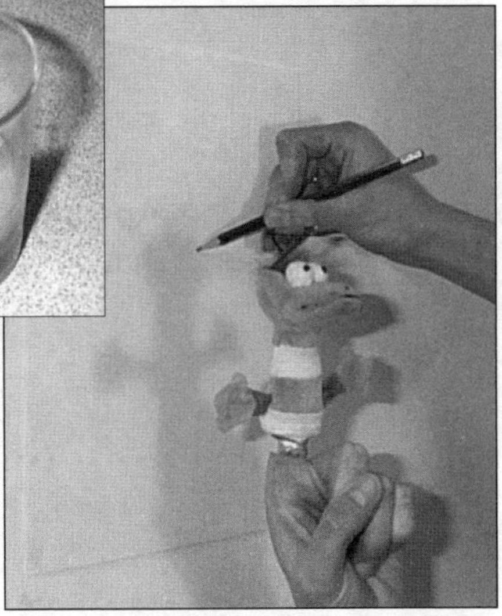

FIRST NAME	
LAST NAME	
SCHOOL	

CGP

1 Teeth

Shoni was interested to find out which drinks she could have without damaging her teeth. She set up an experiment using egg shell to represent her teeth. She placed some eggs in jam jars. For each jam jar, she poured in a different liquid until the egg was covered. The liquids she used were milk, fizzy pop, water, cordial.

a) She noticed, after one week, that the egg submerged in the fizzy pop had started to crumble. What was happening to the egg?

....

....

1 mark

b) She tried the experiment again, but this time she covered half of the egg with toothpaste. What do you think happened to the egg in the fizzy pop this time?

....

....

1 mark

c) How can we prevent this type of damage happening to our teeth? (Name 2 ways)

i) ....

1 mark

ii) ....

1 mark

2 Plant Cycle

Two children carried out an investigation to test whether plants grow better if they have more water. The children kept four plants in each of the following conditions:

Type of plant	Location	Amount of water given daily
4 Geraniums	On a window ledge	$5cm^3$
4 Geraniums	In a cupboard	$20cm^3$
4 Geraniums	Outside	$50cm^3$
4 Geraniums	In a greenhouse	No water

a) Was the test fair? ....

Explain your answer.

....

1 mark

b) Which two variables need to be kept constant?

☐ Amount of water

☐ Type of plant

☐ Colour of flower

☐ Size of pot

2 marks

c) Why did the children put 4 geraniums in each location?

....

....

1 mark

d) Plants need water in order to grow.
Name something else that plants need to help them grow.

....

1 mark

3 Identifying Materials

a) Trevor and Lisa talked about why different things are made from different materials.

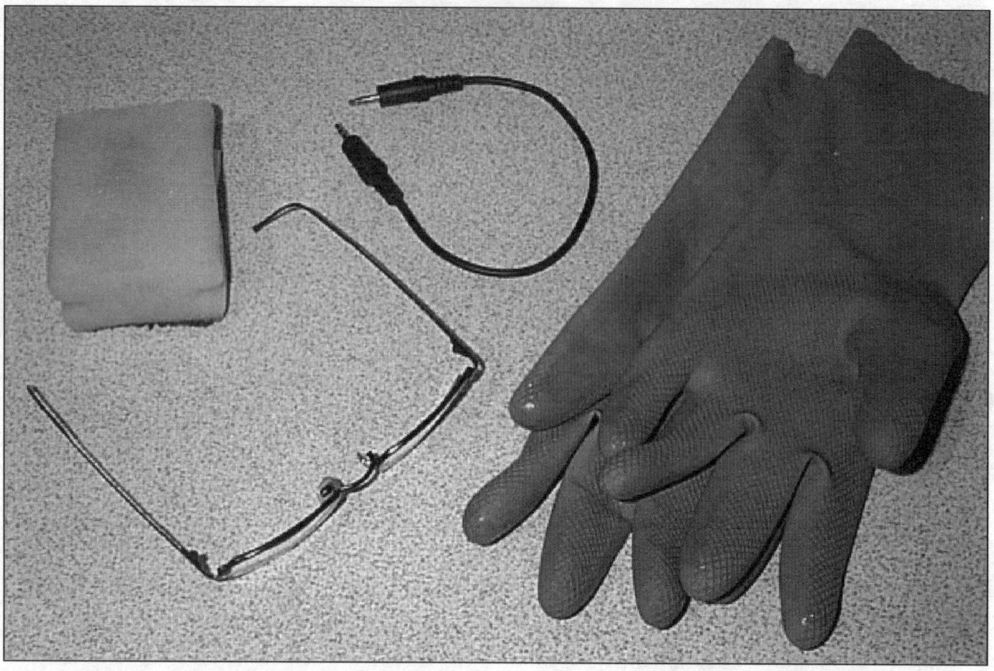

Finish off each of these 3 sentences by writing **ONE** correct letter in each box.

You may only use a letter once.

A — transparent	**B** — waterproof	**C** — an electrical conductor
D — absorbent	**E** — an electrical insulator	

(i) Electrical wires are made from metal because it is ☐ 1 mark

(ii) Glass is used for lenses because it is ☐ 1 mark

(iii) A sponge can be used to wipe up spilt liquid because it is ☐ 1 mark

b) Sally looked at some other materials.

Sally tested the different properties of each material.
She wrote her results in a table.

Complete this table.

The first row has been filled in for you.

Materials	**Properties**			
	conducts electricity	waterproof	transparent	magnetic
pencil lead (graphite)	Yes	Yes	No	No
candle wax	....	....	....	....
steel can	....	....	....	....
copper wire	....	....	....	....

1 mark

1 mark

1 mark

4

Sounds

a) Nigella makes sounds by twanging a ruler on the edge of the table.

Explain why the ruler makes a sound.

....

.... 1 mark

b) How can Nigella make the sound softer?

.... 1 mark

c) How can Nigella vary the **pitch** of the note she makes?

....

.... 1 mark

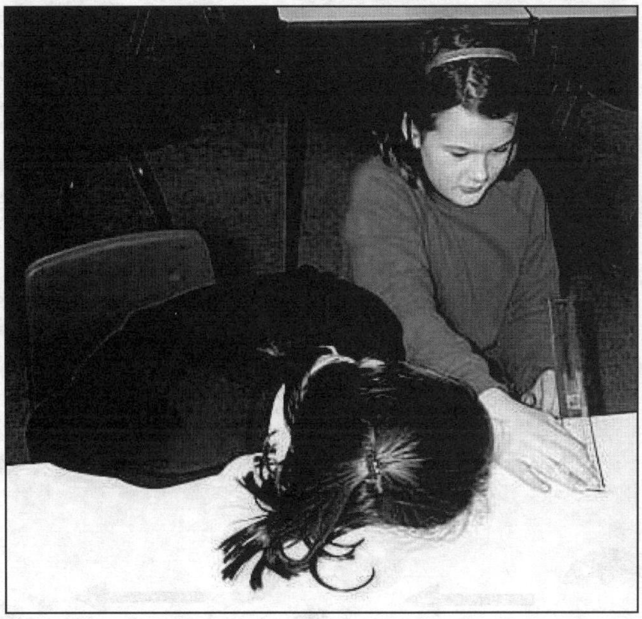

d) Pia puts her head on the plastic desk. Nigella twangs the ruler again.

Pia hears the note it makes. It sounds louder.

Complete the sentence below to explain how the sound reaches Pia's ear.

Tick **ONE** box only.

The sound travels through...

plastic only. ☐

air only. ☐

plastic and air. ☐

1 mark

5

Freshwater River

This is a food chain from a freshwater river.

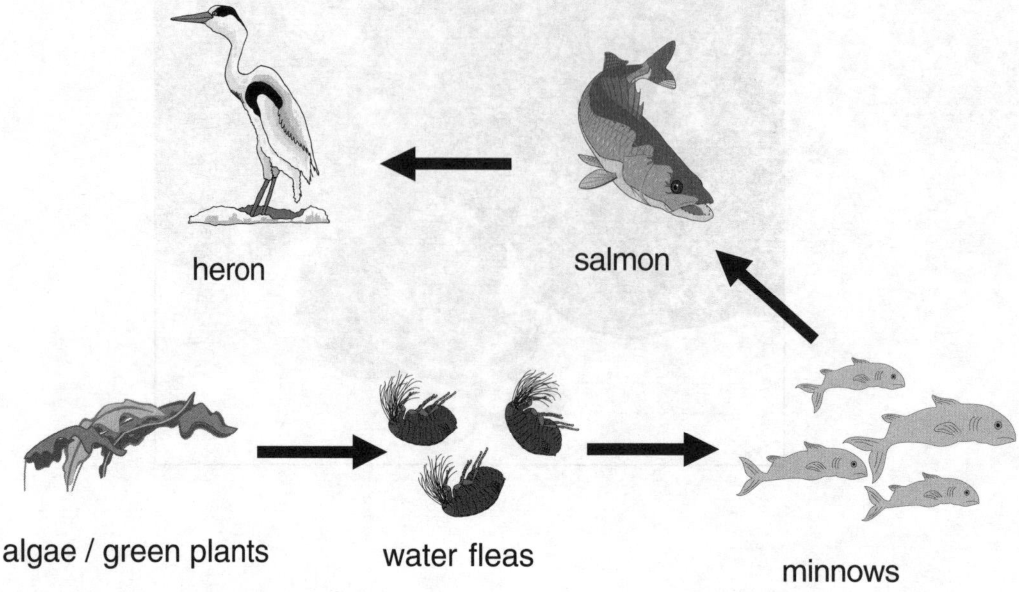

The water flea has long, feathery antennae on its head to help it swim.

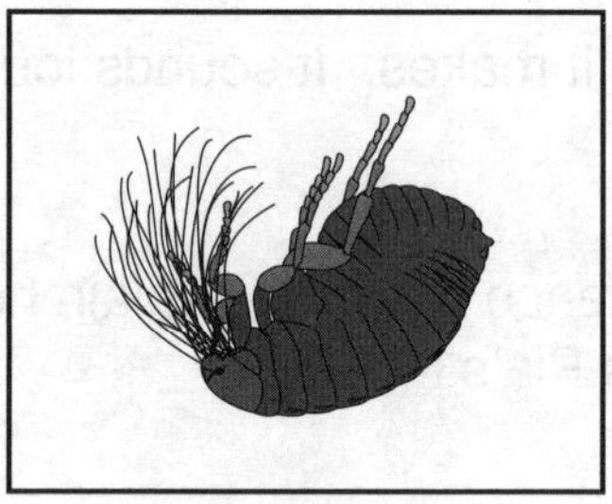

a) What does the heron have to help it catch fish?

....

1 mark

b) What does the salmon have to help it push itself through the water?

....

1 mark

c) What is the **producer** in the food chain pictured opposite?

....

1 mark

d) What would be the effect on the number of herons in this river if **ALL** the water fleas died?

....

....

1 mark

6 Shadows

a) A sheet of clear plastic and a sheet of cardboard are held up between a lamp and a wall.

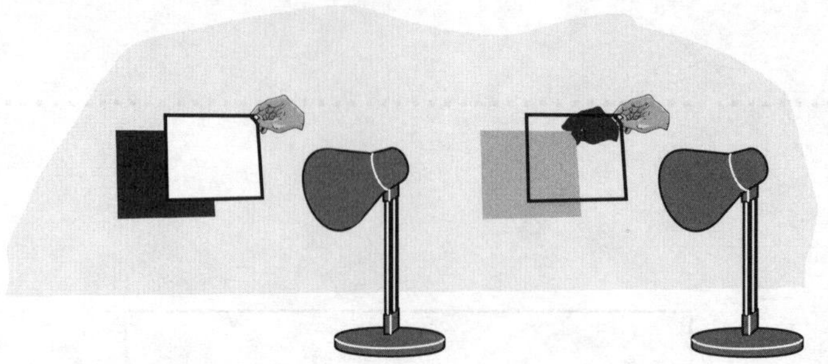

You can see that cardboard makes a **dark** shadow and a sheet of clear plastic makes a **faint** shadow.

Explain why the shadows are different.

....

....

1 mark

b) Tick the objects in this list which make a faint shadow.

Tick **THREE** boxes.

a piece of tracing paper ☐

a red clay plant pot ☐

a clear plastic beaker ☐

a CD ☐

an empty glass milk bottle ☐

3 marks

c) Bev is drawing around the shadow of the finger puppet.

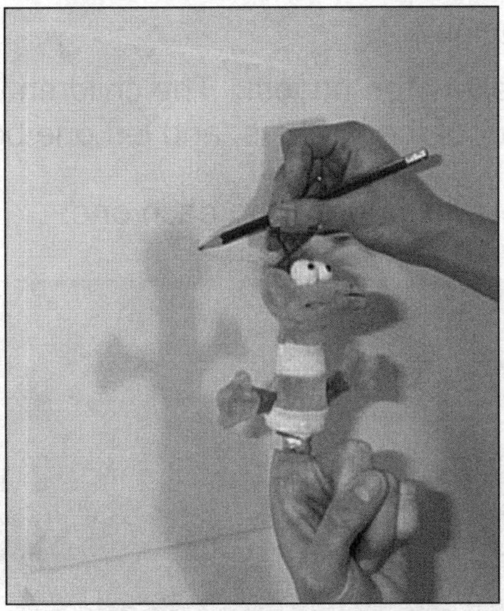

How could Bev make the shadow of the finger puppet bigger?

Tick **TWO** boxes.

move the puppet closer to the paper ☐

use a bigger lamp ☐

move the lamp further away ☐

move the lamp closer ☐

use a brighter lamp ☐

move the puppet closer to the lamp ☐

1 mark

d) **Explain how the puppet's shadow is formed on the paper.**

....

....

1 mark

7 Keeping Things Warm

Some children did an experiment to see which materials were good at keeping things hot.

They used five beakers for the test. The children wrapped a different test material around four of the beakers, and left one beaker uncovered.

100 ml of hot water was poured into each one.

All the beakers were placed in a similar part of the room.

The children timed how long it took for each beaker of water to reach room temperature and used a table to record their results.

Material	How long did the water take to reach room temperature?
newspaper	11 minutes
no cover	3 minutes
polystyrene	14 minutes
polythene bag	6 minutes
aluminium foil	4 minutes

a) Complete this table using **best**, **2nd best**, **3rd best**, and **4th best** to describe how good the different materials are at insulating.

Material	How good was it as an insulator?
newspaper	
no cover	worst
polystyrene	
polythene bag	
aluminium foil	

1 mark

b) Tick the **two** qualities good insulators usually have.

light ☐

heavy ☐

metals ☐

non-metals ☐

2 marks

8

Shadows and the Earth

Aisha stood in the sun in the playground at different times of day and Claire drew her shadow on the ground.

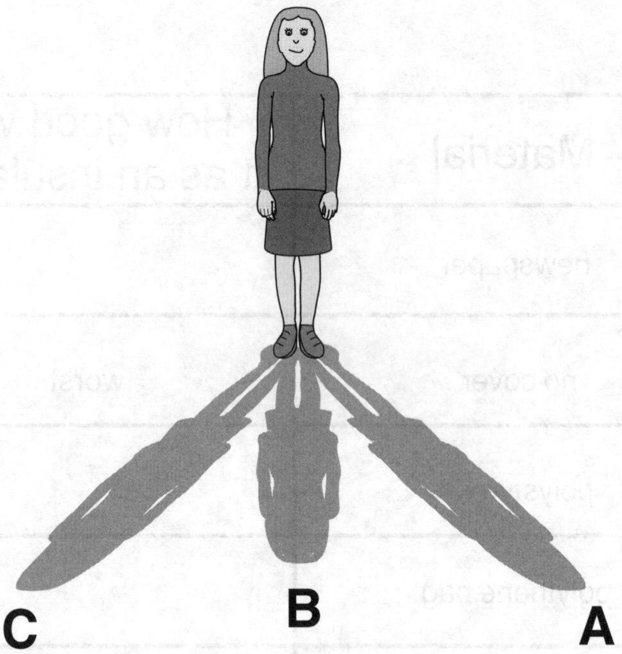

a) What time of day was it at A, B & C?

Choose the right time and write it next to the correct letter.

9 o'clock in the morning

3 o'clock in the morning

midday

midnight

3 o'clock in the afternoon

One has been done for you.

At **A** it is 9 o'clock in the morning.

At **B** it is .... 1 mark

At **C** it is .... 1 mark

b) This diagram represents the Earth and the Sun.

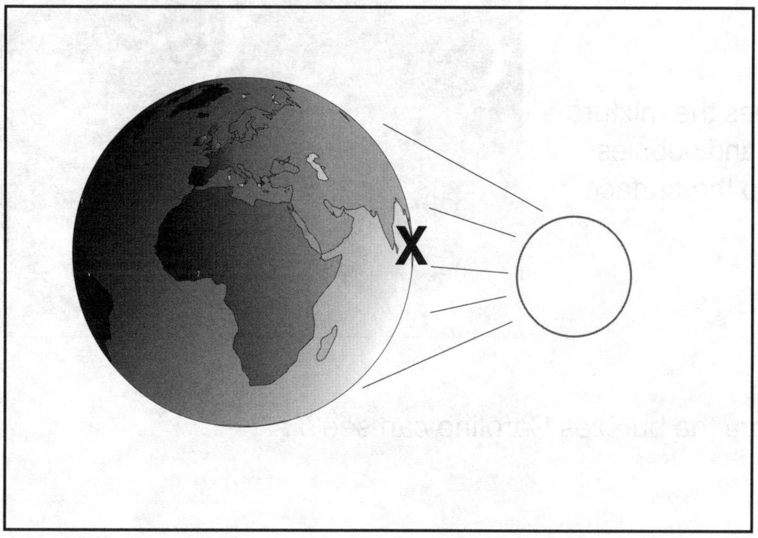

Aisha stands on the Earth at midday in the position marked by the **X**.

Her shadow would be the same as one of the ones shown on the previous page.

Which would be the correct one, **A**, **B**, or **C**?

....

1 mark

c) The Earth spins on its axis.

Explain **ONE** other way that the Earth moves in space.

....

....

1 mark

9 Reactions

Caroline adds some vinegar to some baking soda in a beaker and watches what happens.

She sees the mixture fizzing and bubbles rising to the surface.

a) What are the bubbles Caroline can see?

....

1 mark

b) What is in the beaker? Is it a mixture of vinegar and baking soda or a new substance?

....

....

1 mark

c) Can Caroline separate the baking soda from the vinegar now?

....

1 mark

d) Was this a reversible or irreversible reaction?

Explain why.

....

....

1 mark

shp21 2a

1102

SCIENCE
KEY STAGE 2

Practice Paper 1
Test A

45 MINUTES

TOTAL SCORE

FIRST GO:	
SECOND GO:	
THIRD GO:	

FIRST NAME	
LAST NAME	
SCHOOL	

CGP

1 Parts of a Plant

John wanted to find out what seeds need in order to germinate. He set up an experiment with beans in different locations to test whether light was important. He placed each bean on a wet paper towel on a saucer.

He placed the plants in the following places:

- In a darkened room
- On a window ledge in full sun
- On a table in partial sun

He took care to make sure that the temperature remained the same in each location.

To make his investigation a fair test, he put 4 beans in each location.

a) What do you think the results of John's experiment were? (**Tick one box**)

☐ The plants in the darkened room germinated quickest.
☐ The plants in full sun germinated quickest.
☐ The plants in partial sun germinated quickest.
☐ They all germinated at the same rate.

1 mark

b) Explain your answer.

....

....

1 mark

c) Why is it important for plants to reproduce?

....

....

1 mark

2 **Magnets**

Children tested four things to see if they were magnetic by holding a horseshoe magnet against them to see if they would stick.

They wrote their results in this table.

	Did they stick to the magnet?
Scissors	Yes
Pen	No
Iron Nail	Yes
Pencil	No

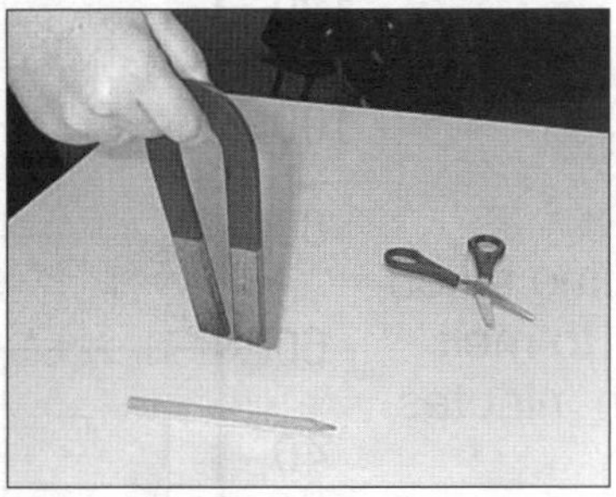

a) Which things were magnetic?

....

1 mark

b) Draw an arrow on this picture to show the direction of the force which is holding the nail to the magnet.

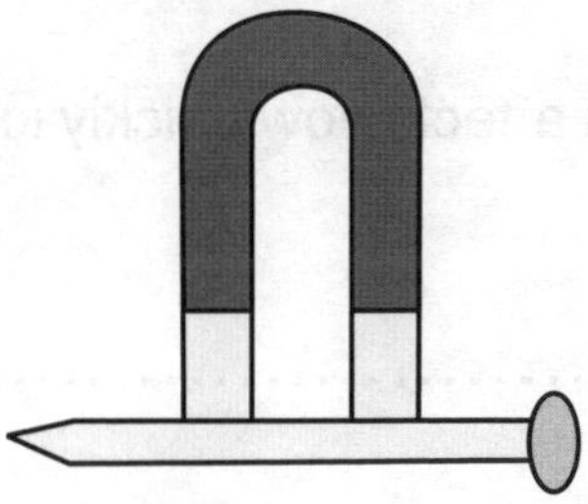

1 mark

c) Explain why the magnet did not stick to the pencil

....

....

1 mark

3 Ice Cubes

Kevin did an experiment with four containers to see which was the best insulated. He put an ice cube in each one and put the lid on. He timed how long it took each cube to melt.

Look at the graph.

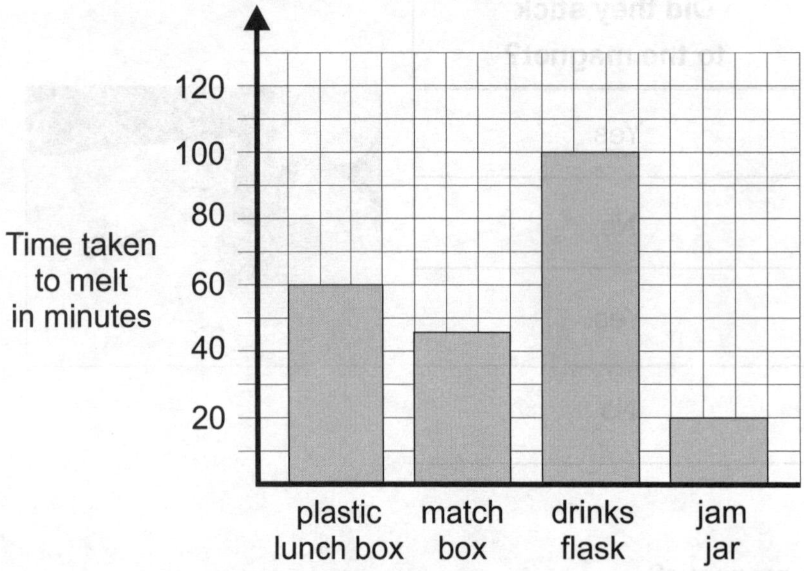

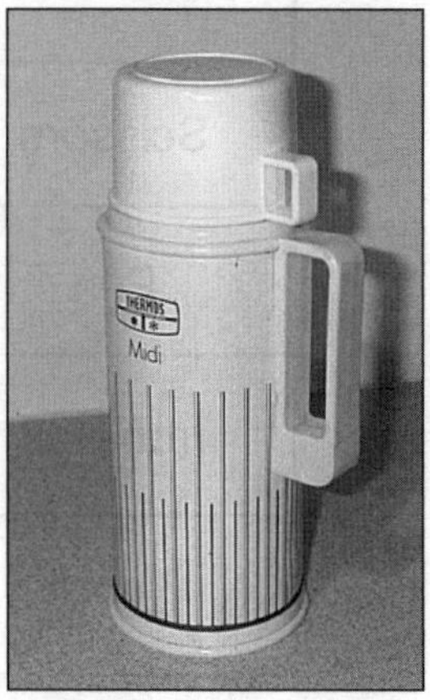

a) Which container was the best insulated?

....

1 mark

b) Describe how insulation affects how quickly ice cubes melt.

....

....

2 marks

c) Write down one thing Kevin should have done to make sure the experiment was fair.

....

1 mark

4 Health

a) **Two** of these sentences about food are true.

Tick the boxes next to the two true sentences.

☐ Rice is full of protein, which gives you energy.

☐ Fruit and vegetables contain lots of vitamins, which keep your cells healthy.

☐ Cakes are mainly made of starch and sugar, which give you lots of energy.

☐ Bread is very fatty, so if you eat a lot, it's good for your heart.

2 marks

b) Dominic has a healthier lifestyle than Chris.

Read the descriptions, and write down two ways in which Dominic's lifestyle is healthier than Chris's.

Dominic
Does exercise three times a week.
Eats lots of fruit and vegetables.
Eats chips at least once a week.
Doesn't smoke.

Chris
Never eats sweets.
Has been a smoker for five years.
Does exercise once a week.
Only eats fruit and vegetables occasionally.

i) Dominic's lifestyle is healthier than Chris's because

....

....

1 mark

ii) Dominic's lifestyle is healthier than Chris's because

....

....

1 mark

5 Soil

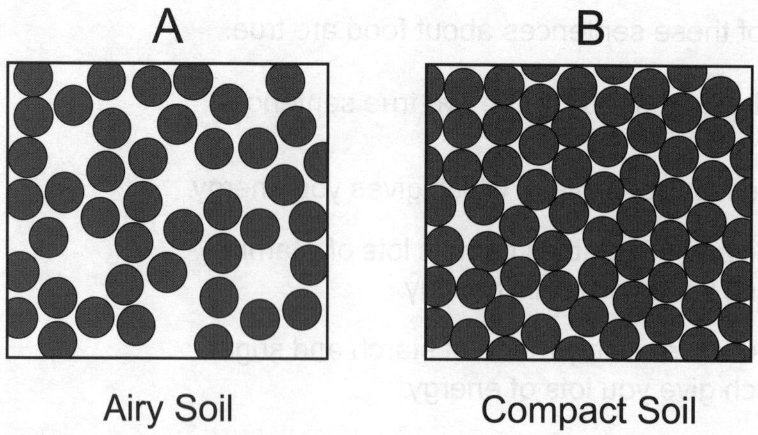

Look carefully at the two different types of soil shown above.

a) Which soil would be a good habitat for a soil-living animal?

☐ A ☐ B

Explain why.

....

....

2 marks

b) Which soil would be best for anchoring plants?

☐ A ☐ B

Explain why.

....

....

2 marks

6 **Electricity**

Some children make a circuit to run an electric fan, using one battery and a fan attached to an electric motor.

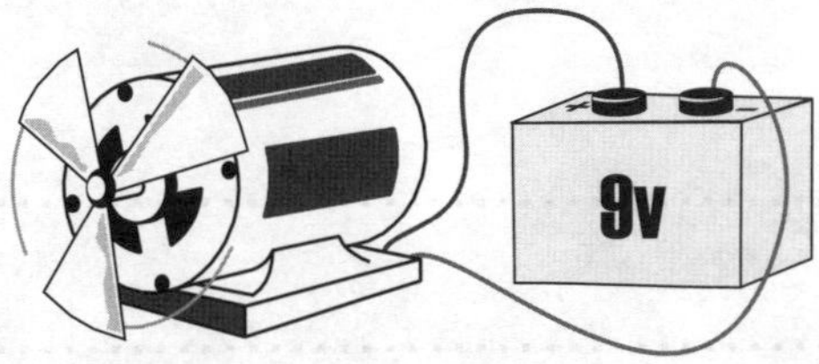

a) **Draw a diagram of the circuit, using just these symbols.**

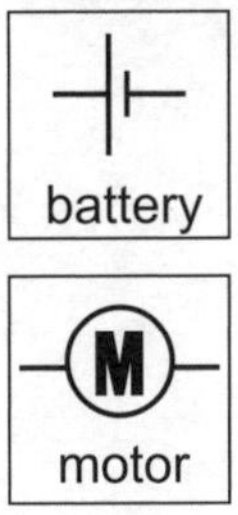

1 mark

b) The children decide to add a switch to turn the fan on and off
It looks like this.

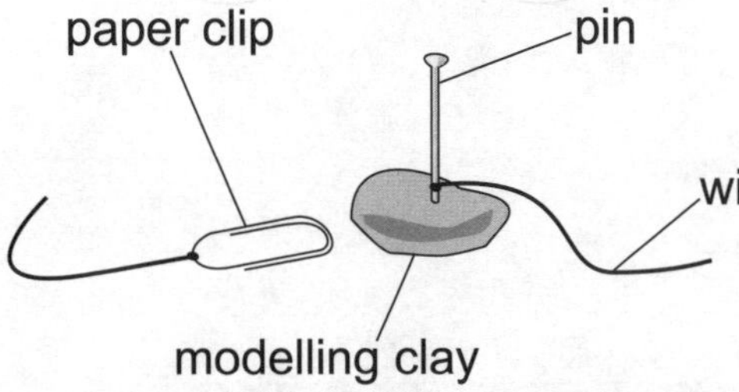

What will happen when the paper clip touches the pin?

....

....

1 mark

c) Explain why this would happen.

....

....

1 mark

d) The children add another fan to the circuit.

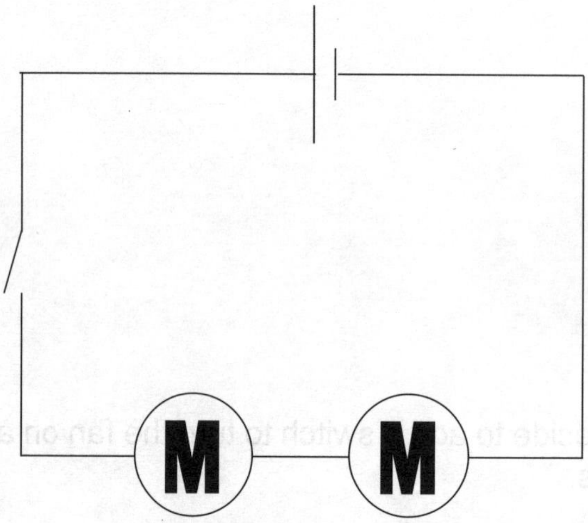

How will this affect the speed of the fan?

....

....

1 mark

7 Temperature

Clara put 100 cm^3 of cold water in a metal pan and heated it till it boiled. She used a thermometer to measure the temperature of the water once a minute, starting when she turned the heat on.

She recorded her results on a graph.

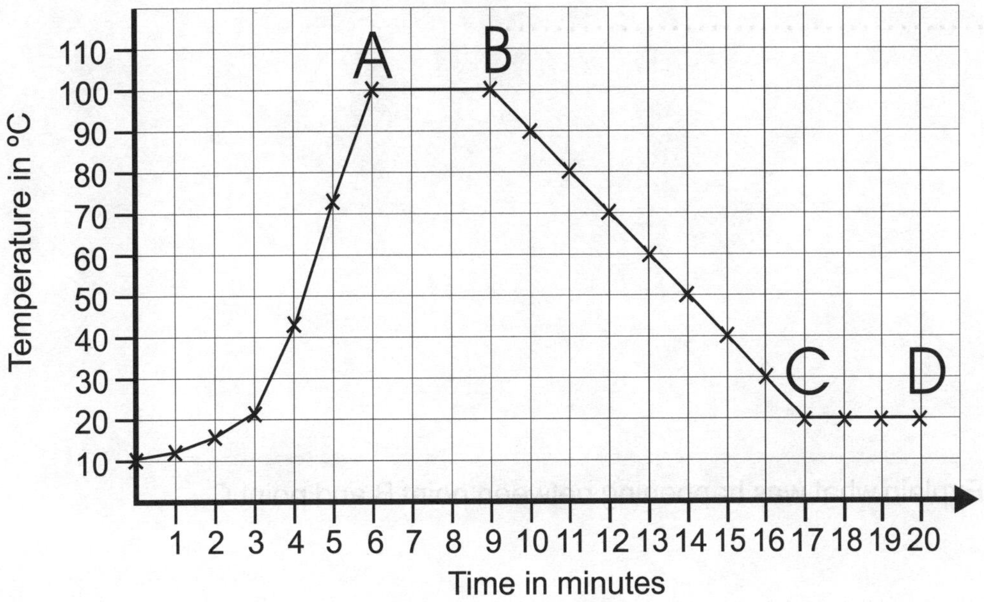

a) What was the temperature of the water to start with?

....

1 mark

b) Which letter shows when the water started boiling?

....

1 mark

c) After the water had been boiling for a short time, Clara turned off the heat.

How long did the water boil for?

....

1 mark

d) Explain what was happening between point B and point C.

....

....

1 mark

e) Clara boiled the water in a metal pan.

Why is metal a good material to make cooking pans from?

....

....

1 mark

8 **Water and Sugar**

a) Simon put 75 cm^3 of water into two separate plastic cups.
The cups were exactly the same size and thickness.
He put one cup into the fridge and one into the freezer.
He left the cups where they were for five hours then took them out.

What do you think happened to the water in the freezer?

....

....

1 mark

b) Simon measured the temperature of the water from the fridge using the thermometer below.

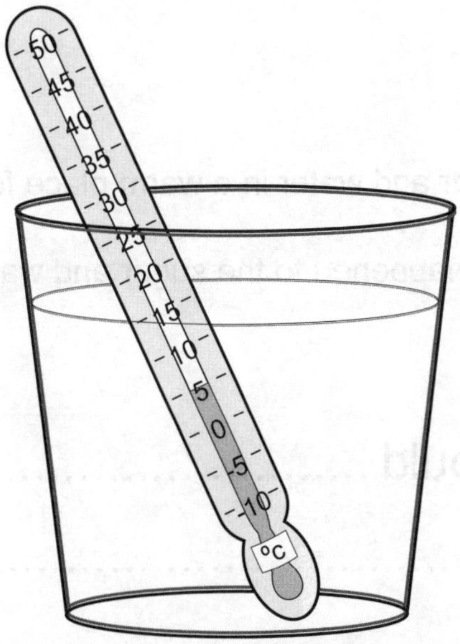

What was the temperature of the water from the fridge?

....

1 mark

c) Simon put 100 cm^3 of water into another beaker and added 10 g of sugar. He stirred the sugar and water until the sugar was completely dissolved.

How did Simon know when the sugar was completely dissolved?

....

....

1 mark

d) Simon left the sugar and water in a warm place for two weeks.

What do you think happened to the sugar and water after two weeks?

The water would ....

....

1 mark

The sugar would..

....

1 mark

9 **Shadows**

The teacher showed Class 6B some photos of the Moon.

A

B

You can't see all of the Moon in photo A because part is covered by a shadow.

a) Explain how this shadow is formed.

....

....

1 mark

b) Here are some more pictures of the Moon.
Look carefully at the dates of these pictures.

3 March

8 March

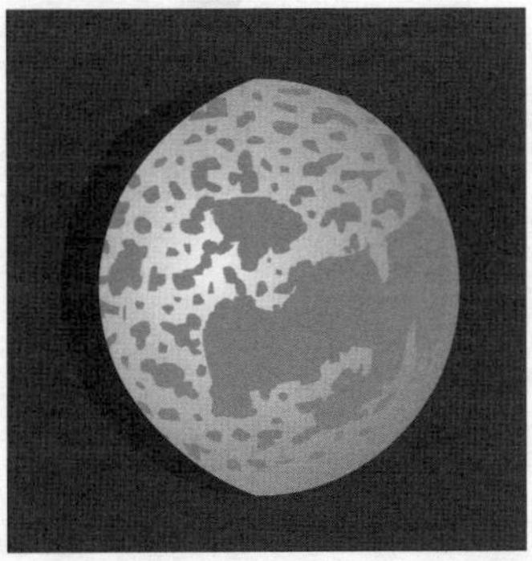

15 March

On what date in March do you think the Moon was full?

Circle the correct date.

1 March   8 March   17 March   22 March   29 March

1 mark

c) The Moon moves around the Earth.
The Sun does not move around the Earth,
but it looks as though it does.

Explain why this Sun **seems** to move around the Earth.

....

....

1 mark

d) These drawings show a lighthouse and its shadow at
8 am, 12 noon, 4 pm and 8 pm.

Fill in the missing labels for these drawings.

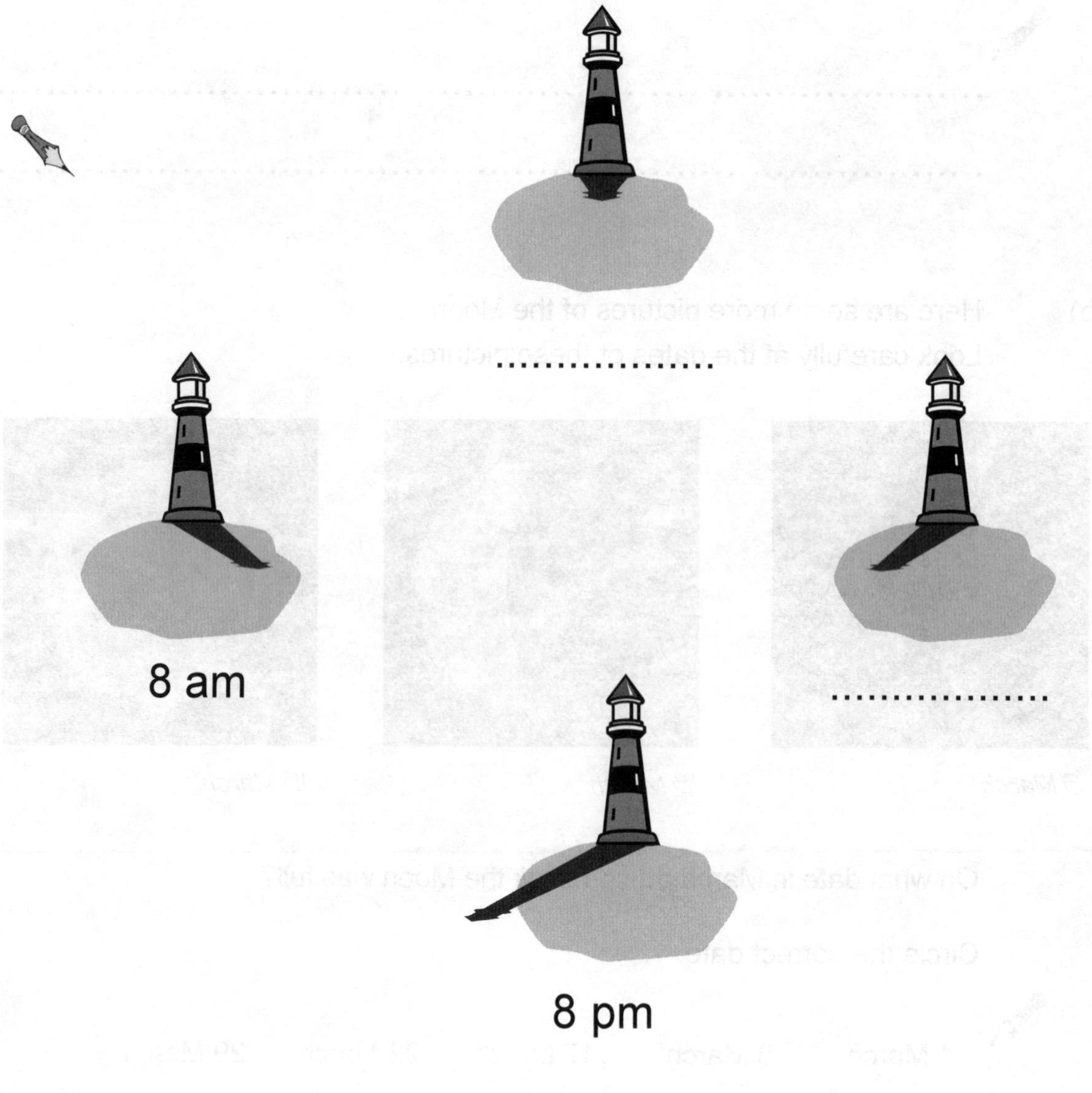

1 mark

1 mark

10 Mould

a) Giles and Sandra put equal-sized pieces of cheese into four clear plastic bags. They left the bags in four different places around the school, and measured the temperature of each one.

After two weeks they made this table to show what had happened to the cheese.

Bag	1	2	3	4
place where cheese was left	window sill	fridge	top of radiator	kitchen cupboard
temperature	16°C	4°C	21°C	12°C
cheese after two weeks	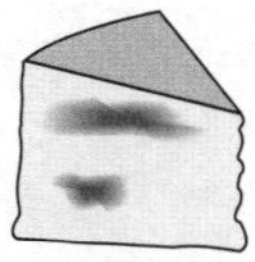			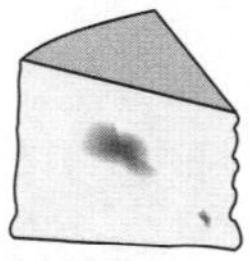

Where was the best place to store cheese to keep it fresh?

....

1 mark

b) **Explain how the amount of mould on the different pieces of cheese depends on the temperature**

....

....

1 mark

1 mark

Coordination Group Publications

Key Stage 2

Science

Answer Book

SATS Practice Papers

Levels 3-5

Contents

Using the Practice Papers........................P2
Answers..P5

These practice papers won't make you better at science

... but they will show you what you **can** do, and what you **can't** do.

The papers are like the ones you'll get on the day — so they'll tell you what you need to **work at** if you want to do **better**.

Do a test, **get it marked** and look at what you **got wrong**.
That's the stuff you need to learn.

Go away, **learn** those tricky bits, then **do the same test again**. If you're **still** getting questions wrong, you'll have to do even **more practice** and test yourself **again**.

It doesn't sound like a lot of **fun**, but it **really will help**.

There are two big ways to improve your score

1) **Keep practising the things you get wrong**
If you keep getting the forces questions wrong, practise forces. If you keep making a hash of the food chain questions, practise food chains. And so on...

2) **Don't throw away easy marks**
Even if a question looks dead simple you have to check your answer and make sure it's sensible.

Doing the Tests

There are **three sets** of practice papers in this pack.

Each set has:

Test A 45 minute test **40 marks**

Test B 45 minute test **40 marks**

There isn't any major difference between the A tests and the B tests.
It's just a way of making you do more questions.

You need these things

A **pen** and a **pencil**.
A **ruler**.
A **rubber**.
Plain paper.

If you're planning to do the practice papers more than once it's a good idea to write your answers on a separate piece of paper.

Answering the questions

Try to answer **all** the questions — but if there's one you **really** can't do, leave it out and move on to the next one. You can always go back to it at the end if you've got time.

Follow all the instructions

1) The pencil means "**WRITE YOUR ANSWER HERE**". Do what they say.

....

2) Pay extra attention to the charts and tables — it's easy to slip up when you're reading them if you're not careful.

3) The most important thing is to **understand** the questions. Read everything really **carefully** to be sure you're doing what they want.

How to Mark Your Paper

It's **easy**. Use the answers in this booklet to mark the answers for each test.

When you've done a **complete** practice paper (Test A and Test B) take the mark out of **40** for Test A, the mark out of **40** for Test B and write them in the table below.

Add them up to get a mark out of **80**:

	Test A score out of 40		Test B score out of 40		TOTAL score out of 80
Paper 1		+		=	
Paper 2		+		=	
Paper 3		+		=	

Once you've got a **mark out of 80**, it's even easier to find out what **level** that is:

TOTAL score out of 80	LEVEL
20 → 41	3
42 → 60	4
61 → 80	5

Important!

Getting Level 3, 4, or 5 on one of these practice papers is **no guarantee** of getting that in the real SAT — **but** it's a pretty good guide.

Practice Paper 1A — Answers

1 a) They all germinated at the same rate. **1 mark**

b) Plants do not need light to germinate. **1 mark**

c) To make new plants of the same variety. **1 mark**

If you didn't get these right, you need to have another look at MAKING PLANTS GROW WELL.

2 a) iron nail, scissors **1 mark**

b)

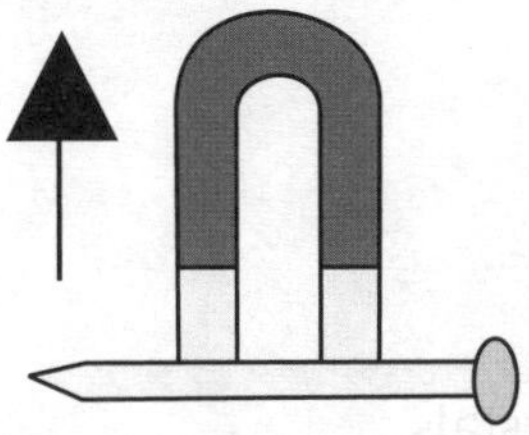

1 mark

The arrow must be vertical and pointing up. Position does not matter.

c) The pencil is not magnetic. **1 mark**

If you got these wrong, you need to do some more work on FORCES.

3 a) drinks flask **1 mark**

b) **2 marks** for The better the insulation is, the longer the ice cubes take to melt. **OR** The worse the insulation is the quicker the ice cubes will melt. **1 mark** for answers like "the ice melts fastest in the best insulated container and slowest in least insulated container" and "the ice melts fastest in the least insulated container" **2 marks**

c) He should have left all the containers in the same place OR he should have used the same size ice cubes each time. **1 mark**

If you made a mess of these, look at KEEPING WARM, and write comparisons with -er words.

4 a) Fruit and vegetables contain lots of vitamins, which keep your cells healthy. **1 mark**

Cakes are mainly made of starch and sugar, which give you lots of energy. **1 mark**

b) i), ii) Two reasons from: he does more exercise; he eats more fruit and vegetables; he doesn't smoke. **1 mark** **1 mark**

If you got these ones wrong, do some more questions on KEEPING HEALTHY.

5 a) Airy soil **A.** It contains more air for the animal to breathe. **2 marks**

b) Compact soil **B.** The soil is harder and more dense which keeps the roots in position better. **2 marks**

If you missed out on the marks, go back and practise questions about LIVING THINGS.

6 a)

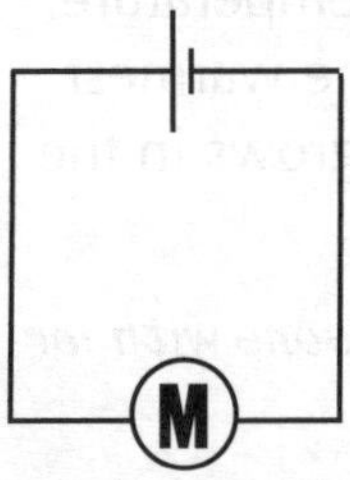

1 mark

b) The fan will turn on. **1 mark**

c) The circuit is closed. **OR** The circuit is complete. **OR** Current/Electricity can flow through. **OR** There's no gap in the circuit. **OR** The switch connects the circuit. **1 mark**

d) The fans will move more slowly. **1 mark**

If you got these wrong, practise questions on ELECTRICITY, especially CHANGING CIRCUITS.

7 a) 10 °C **1 mark**

b) A **1 mark**

c) 3 minutes **1 mark**

d) The water was cooling down. **1 mark**

e) Metal conducts heat well. **1 mark**

If you made mistakes with these, check back over GRAPHS and MEASURING.

8 a) The water froze. **OR** The water turned to ice. **1 mark**

b) 5 °C **1 mark**

c) He could not see any sugar grains in the beaker. **1 mark**

d) The water would evaporate. **1 mark**

The sugar would be left in the beaker. **OR** The sugar would form crystals. **1 mark**

If you made a mistake with these, do more work on CHANGING STATE and DISSOLVING.

9 a) The Moon casts a shadow on itself by blocking some of the light from the Sun. **OR** The Moon blocks some of the Sun's light. **OR** The Moon is opaque. **OR** The light can't get to that part of the Moon because the rest of the Moon blocks it out/is in the way. **1 mark**

b) 17 March **1 mark**

c) The Sun appears to move because the Earth spins. **1 mark**

d)

12 noon 4 pm

2 marks

If you lost out on the marks, you need to look at EARTH, SUN AND MOON.

10 a) fridge **1 mark**

b) **2 marks** for: More mould grows when the cheese is kept in a warmer place. **OR** Less mould grows when the cheese is kept in a cooler place. **OR** The higher the temperature, the more mould grows. **1 mark** for answers like "The most mould grows in the warmest place". **OR** "The least mould grows in the coldest place and the most mould grows in the warmest place". **2 marks**

If you got them wrong, do more work on MICRO-ORGANISMS, and writing comparisons with -er words.

Practice Paper 1B — Answers

1 a) On average, the circumference of an adult's head is larger than a child's. **1 mark**

b) For example: i) Use children of the same age / use adults of the same age **1 mark**

ii) Choose children of the same sex / make sure all measurements are made in the same way. **1 mark**

If you didn't get them right, look at MOVING AND GROWING.

2 a) Any reasonable suggestion, eg place a snail in an airy container with a choice of food types. Or observe which food source the snail prefers. (Preferable if experiment is repeated with a few different snails.) **1 mark**

b) Will vary according to the experiment selected, eg same snail, same type of snail, same food types for each snail, same conditions, etc. **1 mark**

c) Type of food. **1 mark**

If you got the got these questions wrong, look at FAIR TESTS.

3 a) i) The sand helps stop the candle from falling over. **1 mark**

ii) If the candle does fall over the sand won't burn and spread the fire. **1 mark**

b) Thick cloth is a good insulator. **OR** It does not conduct heat (well). **OR** It keeps the heat away from the person's hands. **OR** It stops you burning your fingers. **1 mark**

c)

Food	Change when heated	Is the change reversible?
peanut	singes and burns	no
butter	melts	yes
egg yolk	goes pale and hard	no
flour	goes brown	no

1 mark

Got any wrong? Do some more questions on IRREVERSIBLE CHANGES and on KEEPING WARM.

4 a) The sofa blocks the light from the lamp. **1 mark**

b) reflection **1 mark**

c)

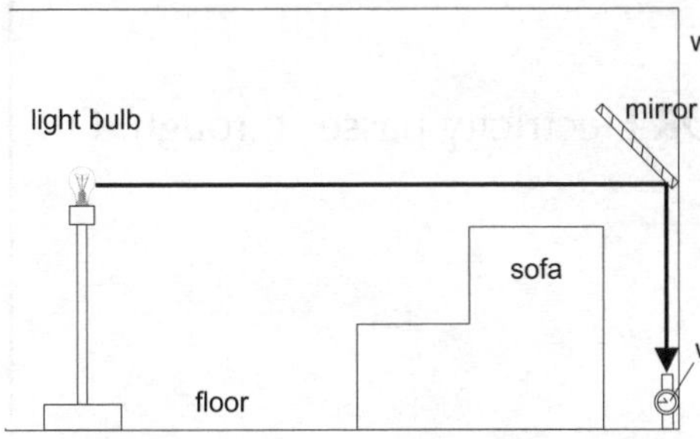

1 mark *for straight ray lines.*
1 mark *for arrow pointing in correct direction.* **2 marks**

If you got the answers or the diagram wrong, do more work on SHADOWS and HOW WE SEE.

5 a) Rain is a **liquid**. Water vapour is a **gas**. Snow is a **solid**. **1 mark** for 2 right answers, no mark for only one correct. — 2 marks

b) Reading from top to bottom, 4, 2, 5, 1, 3. — 1 mark

c) evaporation — 1 mark

If you got these questions wrong, work on CHANGING STATE and the WATER CYCLE.

6 a) i), ii) Any two from: light **OR** water **OR** nutrients. — 2 marks

b) The stem carries water and nutrients to all parts of the plant. — 1 mark

c) The leaves absorb light from the Sun, and use it to make food/sugar **OR** The leaves photosynthesise. **OR** The leaves feed the plant. **OR** They let water escape. **OR** They take in gas/air. **OR** The leaves respire. (Not in KS2, but correct) **OR** The leaves store food. — 1 mark

d) consumer — 1 mark

If you lost out on some of the marks, practise HELPING PLANTS GROW WELL.

7 a) gravity **OR** weight — 1 mark

b) friction — 1 mark

c) paper — 1 mark

d) They need to use the same box each time to make sure the test is fair. **OR** A different box might need less force to move it. **OR** A different box might not give the same results **OR** A different box might be more slippy. — 1 mark

If you got any wrong, do more work on FORCES and FAIR TESTS.

8 a) The piglets weigh twice as much (on the 18th of May) as they did when they were born. — 1 mark

b) Feed, reproduce, grow: **1 mark** for each. — 3 marks

c) **For 2 marks**, The longer the pregnancy is, the bigger the babies are. **OR** The shorter the pregnancy the smaller the babies. For **1 mark**, a statement like "A large baby means a long pregnancy" or "the shortest pregnancy means the smallest babies" — 2 marks

If you missed out on the marks, practise writing comparisons with -er words.

9 a)

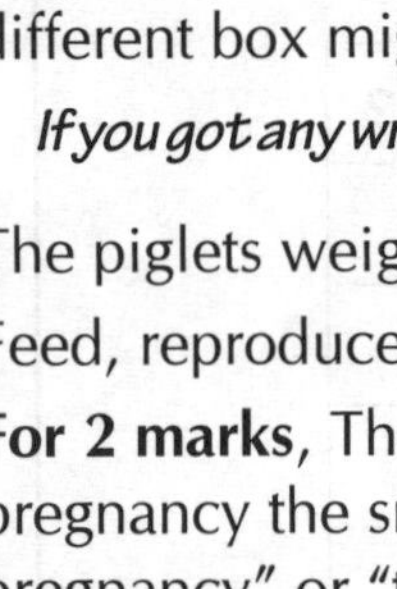

— 1 mark

b) Electricity can flow round the circuit and power the bulb. **OR** Electricity passes through. **OR** It makes a full circuit. **OR** There is no gap in the circuit. — 1 mark

c) Add another battery. — 1 mark

If this was difficult, you need to practise CIRCUITS questions.

10 a) Fine salt dissolved the fastest. — 1 mark

b) To make sure that her results were about the same each time. **OR** To make sure of her results. **OR** To see if the times were right. No mark for "to be exact/accurate" — 1 mark

c) **2 marks** for The larger the grains of salt are the longer it takes them to dissolve. **OR** The smaller the grains of salt are the less time it takes them to dissolve. **1 mark** for answers like "Small grains dissolve the fastest" — 2 marks

If you got it wrong, practise DISSOLVING, FAIR TESTS, and writing comparisons with -er words.

Practice Paper 2A — Answers

1 a) The egg was attacked by acid/sugar in the fizzy pop. **1 mark**

b) The half of the egg covered in toothpaste would not be attacked as much as the half without. **1 mark**

c) For example: Brush teeth regularly;
Use toothpaste;
Visit the dentist regularly;
Avoid foods containing too much sugar. **2 marks**

If you got these wrong, have another look at TEETH and EATING.

2 a) No. The location of the plant changed, therefore other factors will affect the result, eg the amount of light. **1 mark**

b) i) Type of plant.
ii) Size of pot. **2 marks**

c) To ensure a fair test. A plant could have died anyway due to other factors, eg disease. **1 mark**

d) For example: Warmth, light, air, nutrients. **1 mark**

3 a) (i) C. (ii) A. (iii) D. **3 marks**

b)

Materials	Properties			
	conducts electricity	waterproof	transparent	magnetic
pencil lead (graphite)	Yes	Yes	No	No
candle wax	No	Yes	No	No
steel can	Yes	Yes	No	Yes
copper wire	Yes	Yes	No	No

3 marks

4 a) Because it's vibrating/it vibrates. **1 mark**

b) By twanging with less force/more gently. **1 mark**

c) By varying the length of the ruler on/off the table. **1 mark**

d) The sound travels through plastic and air. **1 mark**

Miss out? Look back over SOUND.

5 a) a long beak **OR** long legs **OR** a light coloured body **1 mark**

b) fins **OR** a strong tail **1 mark**

c) algae / green plants **1 mark**

d) There would be fewer herons, possibly none at all. **1 mark**

If you made a mess of this, you need to do more HABITAT and FOOD CHAIN questions.

6 a) Translucent materials let through more light than opaque ones. **OR** The cardboard is opaque but the plastic is translucent. **OR** The plastic sheet is see-through and the cardboard isn't. **OR** The plastic sheet is see-through, so it lets more light through. **OR** The cardboard doesn't let any light pass through it, but the plastic lets quite a lot of light pass through. **1 mark**

b) a piece of tracing paper, a clear plastic beaker, an empty glass milk bottle **3 marks**

c) move the lamp closer, move the puppet closer to the lamp **1 mark**

d) The puppet blocks some of the light and stops it reaching the paper behind. **OR** The light cannot go through the puppet. **OR** The puppet is opaque. Answer must use word 'opaque' or refer to light being blocked and not reaching the paper. **1 mark**

If you didn't get them all right, do some more practice on SHADOWS.

7 a)

Material	How good was it as an insulator?
newspaper	2nd best
no cover	worst
polystyrene	best
polythene bag	3rd best
aluminium foil	4th best

1 mark

b) light, non-metals **2 marks**

If you made a mess of it, you need to do more KEEPING WARM questions.

8 a) At **B** it is midday. At **C** it is 3 o'clock in the afternoon. **2 marks**

b) **B** **1 mark**

c) The Earth orbits the Sun. **1 mark**

If you got them wrong, do some EARTH, SUN AND MOON questions.

9 a) bubbles of gas **1 mark**

b) It is a new substance. **1 mark**

c) no **1 mark**

d) It is an irreversible reaction because you can't make vinegar and baking soda from what is left. **1 mark**

If this was difficult, you need to practise IRREVERSIBLE REACTIONS.

Practice Paper 2B — Answers

1 a)

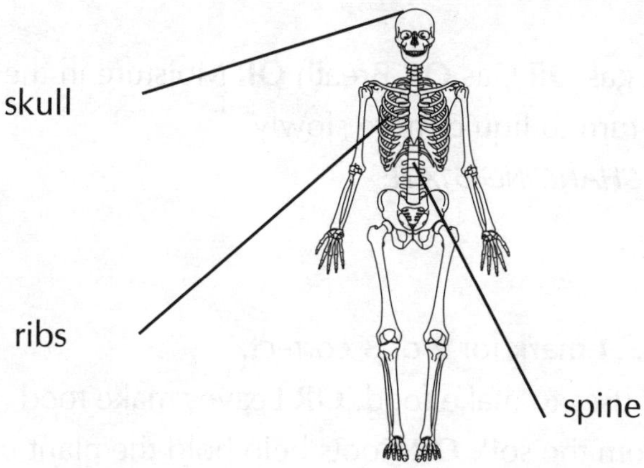

Accept rib cage for ribs. Accept cranium for skull. Accept vertebra or backbone for spine. If two are correct, give **1 mark**. If only one is correct, sorry but **no mark**. **2 marks**

b) i) and ii) Give **1 mark** for each answer from these categories. For **2 marks**, answers must come from different categories: **Movement** — The skeleton helps us move/run/etc. **OR** The skeleton has joints so you can move. **Support** — The skeleton helps you stand up. **OR** It gives the body shape. **OR** Muscles are attached to the skeleton. **Protection** — It protects organs. **OR** The ribs protect the heart. **OR** The skull protects the brain. **Blood** — It makes red blood cells (not in KS2 teaching, but is correct). **2 marks**

c)

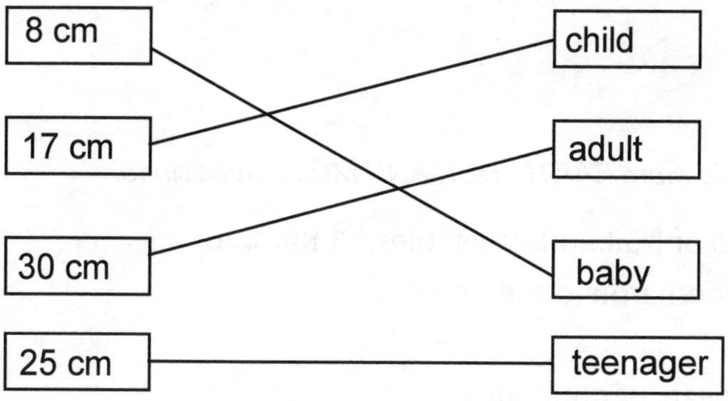

1 mark

If you didn't get them right, you need to practise MOVING AND GROWING, and LIFE CYCLES.

2 a) Shelf above the radiator **1 mark**

b) 837 ml **1 mark**

c) Micro-organisms need warmth to grow well. **1 mark**

d) For example:
- Store item in fridge/freezer
- Keep food covered
- Heat food properly when cooking to kill micro-organisms
- Preserve foods properly
- Wash hands
- Don't sneeze or cough over people.

2 marks

If this caught you out, you need to look at MICRO-ORGANISMS.

3 a) Foam padding **1 mark**

b) Ear muffs are often made with foam padding. Soft surfaces absorb the sound. Any other sensible answer accepted. **1 mark**

c) Sound is vibrations which travel to our ear (it travels through solids, liquids or gases). **1 mark**

If you got it wrong, you should do more SOUND questions.

4 a) Melting. No marks for any other answer. **1 mark**

b) The air **OR** Water vapour **OR** Water as a gas **OR** Gas **OR** Breath **OR** Moisture in the air **1 mark**

c) The ice cubes in the second glass would turn to liquid more slowly. **1 mark**

If you missed out on the marks, practise CHANGING STATE.

5 a) **1 mark** for answers between 23 and 27 cm **1 mark**

b) **1 mark** for answers of 29, 30 or 31 days **1 mark**

c) Reading from top to bottom — E, D, F, B. **1 mark** for 2 or 3 correct. **2 marks**

d) i) Leaves absorb sunlight which the plant uses to make food. **OR** Leaves make food. **1 mark**

ii) Roots take in moisture and nutrients from the soil. **OR** Roots help hold the plant up. **1 mark**

If you didn't get them all right, you need to do more work on LIFE CYCLES and PLANTS.

6 a) Newtons **OR** N **1 mark**

b) The brick was hardest to move. **1 mark**

c) Gravity **OR** weight **1 mark**

d) Friction **1 mark**

If you got these wrong, practise FORCES questions.

7 a) The Earth goes/spins round on its own axis. **OR** It moves because the Universe is expanding. **1 mark**

b) 1 year **1 mark**

c) At B it is sunrise. At C it is morning. **2 marks**

If you got these wrong, you need to do more EARTH, SUN AND MOON questions.

8 a) Doing exercise every day, eating lots of fruit and vegetables. **1 mark** for each. **2 marks**

b) The heart pumps/sends/circulates blood around the body. **1 mark**

c) Arteries **1 mark**

d) Accept anything between 70 to 78 beats per minute. **1 mark**

e) Answer must say that after resting, heart rate goes back down to resting rate (or near resting rate). No mark for incomplete answer "because she rested" "because it's always the same". **1 mark**

Missed out on some of the marks? Do some practice on KEEPING HEALTHY.

9 a) All the containers were the same **OR** They left the containers in the rooms for the same amount of time **OR** The containers all started with the same amount of water. **1 mark**

b)

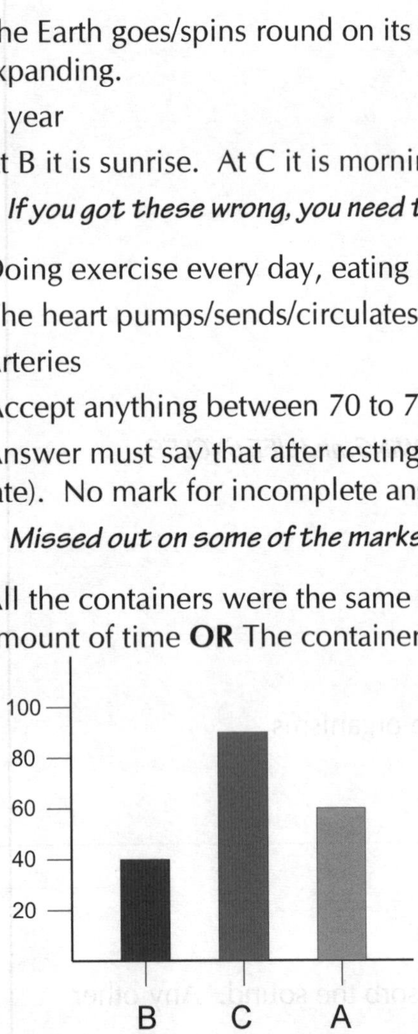

1 mark

c) "The warmer the room, the more water evaporates," for **2 marks**. An answer like "More/most water is left in a cool room," gets **1 mark**. **2 marks**

If this stumped you, practise EVAPORATION and writing comparisons with -er words.

Practice Paper 3A — Answers

1 a) (i) Fewer people smoked in 1990 than 1980. **OR** More people stopped smoking. **OR** It has gone down. **OR** It has gone from 40% to 35%. **1 mark**

(ii) They have realised that smoking is unhealthy. **OR** They have learned that it is bad for them. **OR** There are health warnings on the packets. **OR** Cigarettes became more expensive. **1 mark**

b) Erica **1 mark**

c) lung cancer **OR** heart disease **OR** emphysema **OR** bronchitis **1 mark**

If you got these ones wrong, you need to do more KEEPING HEALTHY questions.

2 a) One of the batteries is the wrong way round. **OR** The batteries are not both facing the same way. **1 mark**

b)

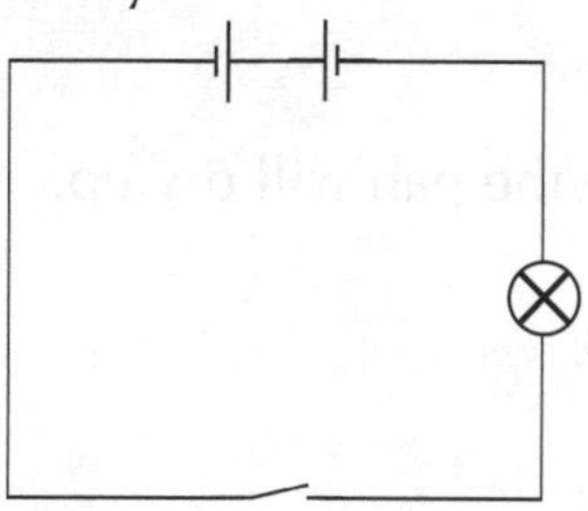

1 mark

or similar circuit diagram.

If this caused problems, you need to practise CIRCUITS.

3 a)

	Pen	Scissors	Pencil sharpener	Die
Made of:	plastic	plastic and steel	steel	wood
Does it float?	yes	**no**	no	**yes**
Is it attracted by a magnet?	**no**	plastic - no steel - yes	yes	**no**

1 mark
1 mark
1 mark
1 mark

1 mark for each right answer.

If you got any of them wrong, you need to do more MATERIALS questions.

4 a) Water melon represents the Sun, orange represents Earth and grape represents the Moon. **1 mark**

b) The Moon orbits the Earth (every 28 days). **1 mark**

c) The Earth orbits the sun (every 365¼ days). **1 mark**

d) 8 am. **1 mark**

e) The sun rises in the East and sets in the West so if the shadow has been cast in a westerly direction, the time must be early morning. **1 mark**

f) Aiden blocked out the light. **1 mark**

5 a) It is vibrating **OR** it makes the air vibrate. **1 mark**

b) The sound will be louder. **1 mark**

c) **For 2 marks** A shorter band will make a higher sound. **OR** A longer band will make a lower sound. **For 1 mark**, answers like "The shortest band makes the highest sound." **OR** "A short band makes a high sound and a long band makes a low sound." **2 marks**

If you got these wrong, do more SOUND questions, and practise writing comparisons with -er words.

6 a) sieving **1 mark**

b) filtering **1 mark**

c) The salt has/is dissolved in the water. **1 mark**

d) The water has evaporated. **1 mark**

e) **For 2 marks** The hotter the heat is, the faster the water will evaporate/the pan will dry up. **For 1 mark**, answers like "If it is hot the pan will dry out quickly" **2 marks**

If you got these wrong, do more questions on SEPARATING MIXTURES.

7 a) moisture/water/warmth/air **1 mark**

b) yellow **1 mark**

c) Still green **OR** not as healthy as the grass around it which hasn't been covered. **1 mark**

d) Two answers from moisture, warmth, nutrients and air. **2 marks**

If you made a mistake, practise KEEPING PLANTS HEALTHY.

8 a) gravity **1 mark**

b) stretchy **1 mark**

c) 6 newtons **1 mark**

d) It would not have the same weight. The water would push up against the sandal, so the effect of gravity would be less. **OR** There is a force (upthrust) pushing up on the sandal. **1 mark**

If you got any wrong, you need to practise FORCE questions.

9 a) 1 mark for box A ticked. **1 mark**

b)

soil	funnel
all clay	B
mostly clay, some sand	C
mostly sand, some clay	D
all sand	A

1 mark

c)

soil	soil type
fastest	E
2nd fastest	A
3rd fastest	D
4th fastest	C
slowest	B

1 mark

If you got these tables wrong, you need to do more on CLASSIFYING MATERIALS and READING DATA.

10 a) 0.95 seconds. **1 mark**

b) The more paper clips, the quicker the spinner fell. **1 mark**

If you got any wrong, you need to practise FORCE questions, especially GRAVITY.

Practice Paper 3B — Answers

1 a) Grow and move. **1 mark** for each.	**2 marks**
b) **1 mark** for a reason given from this list: It has very good hearing. It has very good eyesight. It flies very quietly.	**1 mark**
c) oak tree ⟶ gall wasp ⟶ woodpecker. **1 mark** for correct food chain	**1 mark**
d) The gall wasp is prey. The woodpecker is a predator.	**2 marks**
If you didn't get them all right, you need to practise HABITATS and FOOD CHAINS.	
2 a) The magnets will repel.	**1 mark**
b) Plastic is not magnetic.	**1 mark**
c) **1 mark** for answers in the range 32-36.	**1 mark**
d) They made sure that all the magnets were identical **and** They made sure that all the paperclips were the same size. **1 mark** for each.	**2 marks**
If you missed out on the marks, you should practise MAGNETS questions.	
3 a) The yeast produces gas as it grows.	**1 mark**
b) For **2 marks,** answer must say that David needs to test dough with sugar against dough with no sugar, and warm dough against cold dough. **OR** Otherwise he won't know if it needs both sugar and warmth. **OR** If he only tested sugar and no sugar he wouldn't know if warmth mattered. **OR** If he only tested warm and cold he wouldn't know if sugar mattered. **OR** He needs to test all of the combinations. **1 mark** for 'It needs to be a fair test'.	**2 marks**
c) Sugar and warmth	**1 mark**
If this stumped you, do some more MICRO-ORGANISMS questions, and work on FAIR TESTS.	
4 a) condensation/condense	**1 mark**
b) Cuthbert's breath is hotter than the window.	**1 mark**
If you didn't get them right, you need to do some more work on CHANGING STATE.	
5 a) The bells vibrate **OR** make air vibrate.	**1 mark**
b) The sound travels through the air/atmosphere/gases.	**1 mark**
c) The bells stopped vibrating.	**1 mark**
d) The wool blanket.	**1 mark**
If you got these wrong, do more SOUND questions.	
6 a) The stigma collects pollen from bees.	**1 mark**
b) The petals are large and brightly coloured to attract the bees. **OR** They attract bees.	**1 mark**
c) Wind pollination **OR** pollination by birds or other animals	**1 mark**
d) White campion	**1 mark**
White petals	**1 mark**
If you made a mess of this, practise using IDENTIFICATION KEYS, and look at PLANT LIFE CYCLES.	

7 a) i) The light went through the glass. **1 mark**

ii) The light made the spoon look shiny. **1 mark**

iii) The light was blocked by the pepper pot and it cast a shadow. **1 mark**

b)

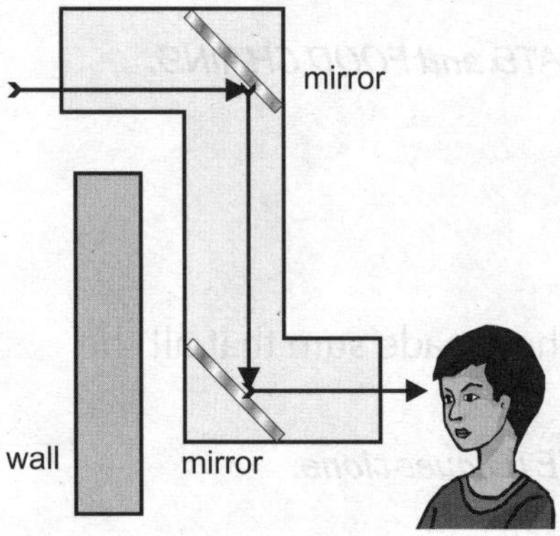

1 mark

If you didn't get this one right, you need to do more work on HOW WE SEE THINGS.

8 a) Gas from the perfume travelled through the air to Andrew's nose. **1 mark**

b) It evaporated. **1 mark**

c) For example: warmth, breeze, surface area. **2 marks**

9 a) The doorbell will not work. **1 mark**

b) Metal conducts electricity. **1 mark**

c)

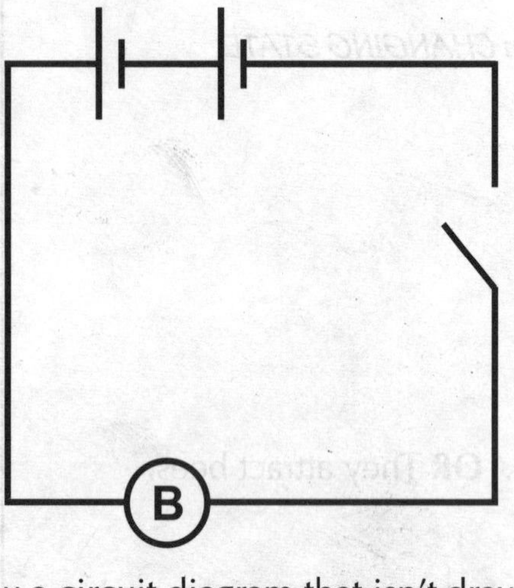

2 marks

Allow a circuit diagram that isn't drawn with straight lines and right angles.

If you couldn't do it, you should practise CIRCUIT questions, especially drawing CIRCUIT DIAGRAMS.

10 a) Wheat Bites **1 mark**

b) It is low in sugar and high in fibre and protein. **1 mark**

If you got these wrong, you need to do more KEEPING HEALTHY questions.